You want to study WHERE?!

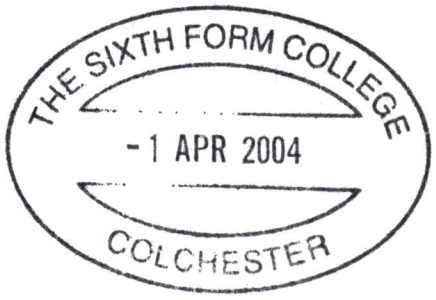

You want to study WHERE?!

Alternative degree destinations

Philip Dring, Barbara Lynn
and Jim O'Brien

trotman

You Want to Study Where?!
This first edition published in 2004 by Trotman and Company Ltd
2 The Green, Richmond, Surrey TW9 1PL

Editorial and Publishing Team
Authors Philip Dring, Barbara Lynn and Jim O'Brien
Editorial Mina Patria, Editorial Director; Rachel Lockhart, Commissioning
Editor; Anya Wilson, Editor; Erin Milliken, Editorial Assistant
Production Ken Ruskin, Head of Pre-press and Production
Sales and Marketing Deborah Jones, Head of Sales and Marketing
Managing Director Toby Trotman

Cover design Pink Frog

British Library Cataloguing in Publication Data
A catalogue record for this book is available from the British Library

ISBN 0 85660 884 X

Typeset by Avocet Typeset, Chilton, Aylesbury, Bucks
Printed and bound in Great Britain by Creative Print & Design Group (Wales) Ltd

Contents

About the authors

Philip Dring is a senior partner at October Associates, one of the UK's leading educational PR consultancies. He spent more than 15 years working in education as a lecturer and manager.

Barbara Lynn is a freelance educational writer and consultant. Until recently she was leader of the Communication Programme Group at Southampton Institute, where she was involved for many years in student exchanges across Europe. She has also taken part in International Labour Organisation (ILO) projects, teaching in polytechnics for female students in Pakistan.

Jim O'Brien is Senior Lecturer and Course Leader in Journalism at Southampton Institute, and co-ordinates the faculty exchange programme. He has extensive experience of developing and implementing international exchange and collaboration programmes in both the UK and overseas. He has lived and worked in the USA, Greece and the Netherlands, and has taught extensively in further and higher education.

Introduction

This guide is about the opportunities that are available to study abroad. It deals with the whole period of your undergraduate studies, as well as the idea of taking time such as a term, or even a full year out, to study overseas. However, it doesn't cover gap years between study at school and university or the option of going abroad to work (although you may well do this while you're studying).

Why go abroad to study?

Studying abroad isn't simply something that students of modern foreign languages do, it's open to everyone. Whatever course you're taking, there's no doubt that the experience will be enhanced by studying abroad, either for a short period or even for the whole of your studies.

Time overseas broadens your horizons, and helps you to understand how other people live their lives in different cultures. Your experience of living abroad is very likely to be different to the brief time you've spent abroad on holidays, which may well have been mostly tourist experiences.

An extended period abroad will mean that you'll encounter different lifestyles. Meeting a new culture means embracing new ideas and ways of thinking, new ways of living and new foods. And the differences can be large or small too. In some cases, countries that seem familiar from holidays can be very different when you live there for a while. For example, in Spain, people have a very distinctive approach to eating – their evening meal doesn't usually begin until around 10pm.

Depending on your outlook, this might seem exciting or even a bit daunting. However, the important thing – and the most important message of this guide – is to think as positively as you can about the opportunities and advantages that studying abroad can bring you.

Chapter 1 deals with the questions you need to ask when you're thinking about study abroad. Chapter 2 goes into the practicalities of applying, with information about schemes such as Erasmus/Socrates. Chapter 3 gives you an A–Z of studying overseas, with information on all aspects of the process.

Chapter 4 offers you a profile of each country, along with case studies of individual universities. More than 20 countries are included, and information is provided on selected universities, giving you a taste of student life in that country.

Finally, there's a list of useful addresses and websites with more information to help you carry out further research.

1
Questions You Need to Ask

Are languages important?

It's possible to study abroad in countries where English is the main language, such as Australia, Canada, Ireland and the USA. As the individual country entries in the directory show, it's also increasingly possible to study in other countries on programmes where the main language is English. This means that you can mix with other students in your destination country who have opted to take their studies in English.

This form of study removes the problems presented by having to learn a foreign language. But it goes without saying that your overseas experience will be improved a lot by learning something of the country's language.

You can get help with this, since overseas universities run language courses specifically for overseas students. More information on this can be found in the individual country entries in this guide.

Why do I need to learn a new language?

One of the main reasons to study abroad is that it can help you to learn a new language, or improve your language skills. The job market is becoming increasingly global, and these skills can be of real benefit to you, improving your prospects. Who would have thought that the English soccer manager would ever have been a Swede, or that leading clubs would be managed by Frenchmen and Italians? Careers advisers in the UK often comment that such skills, particularly knowledge of European languages, are the most important criteria in job selection. If David Beckham can learn Spanish, so can you!

Case study
Learning languages – 1

One thing I discovered whilst abroad is that I enjoy languages and can pick them up fairly quickly – having hated learning German at school, I now learn languages for fun. I have since learnt reasonably serviceable Italian and a smattering of casual Thai; confidence just to try speaking is everything in learning a foreign language, and having done this in one language, you will find it much easier the next time. Your GCSE French will get you a surprisingly long way, if approached with a sense of fun!

Having said that, it can be a challenge for English students. The lack of focus on foreign language tuition in our schools puts us at a slight disadvantage. If you do study abroad, you might find that other students are much happier speaking another language (and probably keen to try out their English on you).

Case study

Learning languages – 2

I found the learning the language aspect quite difficult to start with, especially as the course was very intense and all my lessons were in French. Also the fact that my fellow European students all spoke English to a pretty high standard meant that they wanted to practise English with us, so I always felt we had to make even more of an effort to speak French, as it could have been easy just to let them chat away to us in English.

Their confidence is helped because in some countries, courses make their students work in at least one other language other than their native tongue. For example, many business students in the Netherlands are expected to complete presentations in two languages in addition to Dutch (and if you choose to study in the Netherlands, this may well apply to you).

It's worth remembering that many employers, including the European Union (EU), require most of their employees to be competent in two languages in addition to their own.

Will the education system be the same as in the UK?

When you study overseas, you'll be taking part in a different educational system to the UK (although there are differences in the UK as well). Most undergraduate courses outside of England and Wales take four years (as in Scotland). In many countries, tuition methods are also different to the approach that you may have been used to in this country.

This can often mean that there is greater reliance on lectures with large numbers of students. The German system works in this way, where students are expected to follow up and research on their own to a greater extent than in the UK.

Case study

Teaching styles – 1

My academic contact at the German institution (assigned to keep an eye on exchange students), who was to be addressed as 'Herr Professor', was quite a lofty and distant figure with whom I didn't have much involvement. On one occasion when I was headed for his office, he simultaneously arrived at and entered his office from the opposite direction, and, having seen me, quickly hung a 'do not disturb sign' on his door before I could knock. Know your place as a humble undergraduate! German exchange students in Manchester all commented very favourably on the friendliness of the department.

There are other tuition styles too. In the Netherlands, for example, professional studies function very differently: students work on extended projects that are derived from real business scenarios. In some cases, it's possible to finish an undergraduate programme without needing to write an essay!

How do I decide where to go?

There's more information on this and other differences in the country directory, also case studies of students who have spent time studying abroad, to give you first-hand feedback. The need to think about what method of study best suits you can be an important factor in reaching your decision. It could come down to the way you feel about being able to adapt to a different style of learning. This guide gives you details of how and where you can study in most of the popular destinations, and a few options in less popular places which can offer something different or specialist.

Case study
Making the decision

The decision to study abroad was not easy, I was concerned that I would lose out on what my fellow students were studying in the UK and that I would miss my university life as it was. However, my advice to anyone thinking of studying abroad is to do it! The benefits by far outweigh any doubts you may be having. Challenges will lie ahead, but overall you become a stronger person, and the experience is unforgettable.

Is there any financial help?

This guide will also help you to sort out the best way of going about arranging to study abroad. Chapter 2 goes into this in some detail, but the most likely way will be through one of the schemes that help students to study abroad. The most common is the EU's Erasmus/ Socrates programme – this operates in all the EU countries (there is a list of these countries, including those entering in 2004, on page 12), as well as several other European countries.

The advantage of this scheme is that there can be some modest financial support from the EU to help you fund your studies. It probably won't cover all your costs, but it is reasonably generous. The details can be quite complicated and depend on your circumstances, but generally the scheme allows you to study abroad for a period (usually one term/semester, or one year), and normally in the second year of a three-year undergraduate programme.

In most cases the Erasmus/Socrates programme operates in a formal exchange which is decided by your university and the overseas institution. However, membership of the EU also means that you can apply to study at a university in any of the EU countries. There shouldn't be any fee complications in this situation.

Financial help is much less likely to be available outside the area covered by EU schemes. If you're thinking of studying in one of the Commonwealth countries, the Association of Commonwealth Universities can offer support on researching opportunities, courses and universities. It's worth noting that universities in countries such as Australia maintain websites that are geared towards overseas students.

Beyond this, you'll need to do a little research. Websites are a great resource, but be aware that they're not all maintained to give you the most up-to-date information.

Will my course be recognised in the UK?

Of course, there are always downsides to any idea and study abroad has several. Perhaps the most frequent question that potential exchange students ask is whether there will be any disadvantages to their studies at their own home university if they decide to go abroad.

This shouldn't be a problem if you're going as an exchange student on what is known as a 'bilateral agreement' – this simply means that your own university has signed an agreement with the overseas university. Part of the approval process between the institutions requires them to consider compatibility issues, so that content between courses is interchangeable. Your marks overseas simply count towards your qualification in the UK.

If you're considering taking the whole of your studies abroad, it's a very good idea to check on the acceptance in the UK of the qualifications that you'll gain overseas. This can be particularly important if you want the undergraduate qualification to equip you to work professionally in the UK. This applies especially in subjects such as architecture, accountancy and medicine.

Case study

More than an exchange?

I studied European Management with French at Middlesex University and as part of the course I had to spend the last two years of the four-year course at university in Marseille. During this time I also had to complete a six-month work placement that I ended up doing in Paris. The course was different to Erasmus courses in that my study in France was full-time and I received a French as well as an English degree at the end of the course. The course was therefore more intense than that of friends who'd studied for one year abroad and whose exam marks didn't really contribute to their degree mark.

Safety

Perhaps the most important point to think about, when you're deciding where to study, can be whether or not the country is safe. This guide provides some guidance and includes details of areas defined as being, in differing ways, dangerous. However, new problems can flare up quickly, and in the most unexpected places – until recently, Bali was seen as a safe tourist destination.

The best advice here is to check things before you make your decision. The most up-to-date advice can be found on the UK Foreign Office website (www.fco.gov.uk/). The box in Chapter 3 shows areas that are currently regarded as being dangerous to varying degrees. However, an example of how this can need constant monitoring is that Zimbabwe does not appear on any of these lists, but it was considered too dangerous for the English cricket team to visit in recent months.

Parts of any city can be problematic too, and it's always worth doing your research from up-to-date travel guides – these should give you sound local advice and information. The most obvious piece of advice is simply to be sensible and try to avoid placing yourself in areas and circumstances where you could be at risk.

Case study

A word of warning?

The only complaint that I had was the accommodation. As an exchange can be fairly daunting it is important that exchangees are placed in a nice safe environment. Unfortunately, in Amsterdam this wasn't the case. On the plus side I got used to where I lived, but for some it may have been a bit too unpleasant. The environment for exchangees is important as they need that extra sense of security to ease the feelings of vulnerability and homesickness.

2
What Help Is Available?

If you do decide to go overseas as an independent student, there is likely to be very limited support.

The Association of Commonwealth Universities (ACU)

The Association of Commonwealth Universities maintains information on universities in Commonwealth countries and has a membership of 480 institutions throughout Africa, Asia, Australasia, Canada, the Caribbean, Cyprus, Malta and the South Pacific. It also has some potential to award grants, although competition for these is stiff.

In recent years ACU has developed a student exchange programme – its very helpful website (www.acu.ac.uk) has a section called Commonwealth University Study Abroad Consortium, which gives more information. However, representation from UK universities is a bit thin on the ground.

The ACU also publish the comprehensive *Commonwealth University Yearbook*. This is packed with useful information, but at £200 you'll most likely want to track it down in a library.

If your plans to study abroad independently can't be met from this source, you'll have to follow up with the individual institution concerned. In this guide, there are details about how you can contact individual universities and, where possible, reach country information and clearing centres.

Case study
The real experience – 1
I would have to say that my year spent studying physics in Aachen, Germany, was a life-changing experience. The increased confidence I gained through negotiating this time abroad has subsequently stood me in as good stead, if not better, than the good language skills gained.

Erasmus/Socrates

This is the most likely scheme that you'll come across. As the major European exchange programme covering 30 countries, 120,000 students and 2,000 institutions of higher education, the scheme works through bilateral agreements between institutions in member countries which are usually subject-orientated.

This can be a bit of a problem if, say, you know that your home institution has an agreement with a French university that you really want to go to, but you're studying journalism and the exchange is in business studies. Fortunately, the UK Erasmus Council publishes an annual guide, *Experience Erasmus* (see Useful Addresses and Publications) that gives details of exchanges broken down by both subject and institution. It's clearly a case of doing some homework in advance so that you're not disappointed.

Under bilateral arrangements, while you are away your progress is monitored by your home university, and your grades from the exchange are counted in the same way as if you had been studying in the UK during that time (see details of the European Credit Transfer Scheme (ECTS) – in Chapter 3). In a few cases, institutions do not use ECTS – this is made clear in the Erasmus guide, but be sure to check with your own home institution.

On top of all of this, you may be able to obtain grants from Erasmus to help you with costs. These are only defined as top-up and are not automatically given, but they are helpful and can help in adapting to life overseas.

It goes without saying that while you are on an Erasmus exchange you should be eligible for any student loans that you might be able to claim. You may also be able to get others especially related to the exchange, subject to a means-test.

Almost all the institutions involved in Erasmus exchanges offer incoming students an induction or orientation programme before their studies begin. These can include social events, familiarisation with study techniques and assessment, special arrangements for exchange students (such as courses assessed in English) and language courses.

Other EU schemes

The EU also has exchange cooperation agreements with the US and Canada, and you can find out about these from your home institutions.

The USA

At first sight, the USA seems very promising when it comes to seeking financial assistance. However, it's likely that help will be only partial in cost terms – and competition to get that help is high. The Fulbright Commission is a starting point, in that it provides information about institutions across the US, but most of its financial aid is aimed at postgraduates.

By using the information from the Fulbright you should be able to narrow the field to institutions that offer the right course and those that are likely to be able to offer you financial help. The Fulbright also organises a 'Study in the US' day in October of each year in London, where you can meet representatives from around 100 US higher education institutions – details are available on their website (www.fulbright.co.uk).

Be aware that fee structures can vary dramatically from institution to institution (and information can be quite difficult to find or understand from their websites). Any support is unlikely to cover all your costs though. The guide *Applying to Colleges and Universities in the US* is helpful and has details of where you may be able to apply for financial help. Also worth consulting is College Prospects of America, Inc (www.cpoa.com).

There is also the chance for the sports minded to apply for a sports scholarship – the guide *Sports Scholarships and College Athletic Programs in the US* is very helpful (see Useful Addresses and Publications for details on all of the above).

Most US universities have study–work arrangements, especially on-campus work, which can help you in terms of living expenses; but it's worth remembering that working while you're studying can present issues in terms of organising your time.

Other options

If you want to study abroad, you can also choose a course that is based in the UK which has a period overseas already built into it (often an additional year). Often, foreign language courses have this option, but the range is not limited only to these courses. For example, taking American studies can give you the opportunity to study in the US for a period. However, you should check whether this is an automatic part of the course, or whether it's arranged on a competitive and selective basis. Also, it's a good idea to check where you're likely to be sent. As your course would last for an additional year, you need to consider the impact of student fees and other costs. Details are available from individual institutions and through the UCAS website and directory.

Case study

Long-term benefits

Though I passed all my courses in my year away, I had the luxury of being able to view it as a German-learning exercise first, a physics learning exercise second. I decided that it would be a waste to come home not having learnt the language as well as possible. Nine years later my German is still good, and regularly of use in my professional and personal lives.

3
An A–Z of Studying Abroad

Accommodation

When you land in the new country, you'll need somewhere to live. Your best point of contact is likely to be the university, which may have an accommodation office dealing with lodgings and halls of residence. It's worth bearing in mind that in many countries, students go to their local university and live at home, so there's little need for this facility. In this situation, you may be better off looking for accommodation with a local family (there are agencies that deal with student rentals and placements). In many countries there are also special advice centres for young people that can help with accommodation issues. (More information about what is likely to be available is in the country directory entries.) It's also worth noting that halls of residence may be different to what you may have come to expect or be used to in the UK. Accommodation could be in dormitories, and it's possible that you might not have much private space.

Case study
Learning experiences

Living in a foreign country is quite liberating – as you are a foreigner, few people have expectations of how you will act, and most will be interested to meet you; it is a good opportunity to really define yourself. If you can be quite extrovert during your time, you will get more out of it; language skills are after all about communication, so communicate you must, the more the better! Of all your years spent at university or college, the year spent abroad is not the right one to spend as a shrinking violet in your room.

Adjusting to being abroad

Apart from the initial culture shock, research has shown that we often go through four key stages as we learn to live in a new environment. At first, we're fascinated by our new surroundings – everything is fresh, and we enjoy the difference. But because of this, we don't really engage with the new culture. This may move on to a period of resentment and aggression, where we begin to engage and have a feeling of shock about how different things actually seem. This is a critical time as it can (in extreme cases) lead to rejection and return home, or more positively it can signal moving on to acceptance and adjustment. Acceptance is the third stage, when you're absorbed enough into the new culture to feel comfortable and happy. The final stage is one of adaptation – you've adjusted to the new culture.

Case study
Adjusting to new circumstances – 1
Students need to be aware that at times it can be very hard to be in a foreign country where no one seems to understand you and that it is important to be strong and to get through those hard times, as it will definitely be worth it.

Alcohol
Rightly or wrongly, drinking is seen as an important aspect of British youth culture, although this isn't a shared view throughout the world. Access to alcohol is less restricted in terms of licensing legislation across much of central and southern Europe, but there tends to be less tolerance of drunken behaviour.

In Scandinavian countries, access to alcohol is much more restricted and high taxes can make it too expensive. Also, in some US states and parts of Canada, access to alcohol can be severely restricted and is often restricted to people over 21. In Moslem countries, any access to alcohol can be forbidden (see 'Culture' and 'Religion').

Applications
(See 'How to Apply' and 'When to Apply'.)

Banking
It's important to know about the banking arrangements in the country where you plan to study. (This guide gives some broad details under the individual country entries.)

Case study
Adjusting to new circumstances – 2
Initially it was a culture shock adjusting to university life in Marseille. Also, finding somewhere to live and practical things such as opening a bank account, having the necessary documentation to be able to rent an apartment, etc, were quite tedious. For example, you couldn't open a bank account without having an address and vice versa, and you needed a bill in your name...

Budgeting
You'll find details elsewhere in this guide about how to manage your money and some indication of the cost of living in countries around the world. However, this is only part of the process of budgeting. For some, student life in the UK is tough enough already, and it's worth taking time to think carefully about how much your overseas studies may add

to your financial situation.

This can mean taking a pretty hard-headed approach to living within your means. Being abroad, naturally you'll want to take advantage of travelling or visiting interesting sites, but be sure to find out how much it'll cost before you blow your cash!

It's wise to make contingency plans too: think about putting aside an emergency fund, in case you have to make an unplanned visit back home.

Eating and Budgeting

The best way to eat well and cheaply abroad is to buy local produce. This can mean shopping at markets. Also, look out for places to eat used by local students as usually these will be good value, both financially and nutritionally.

The biggest mistake that UK students make is the 'Marks & Spencer effect', which was noticed by a major exchange programme organiser in the Netherlands. British students spent the first month using the expensive food halls at the Marks & Spencer in The Hague. There was clearly a comfort factor here, in that the shop provided familiar food. But after a month or so, students had moved on to using local and cheaper produce.

Culture

Part of the pleasure of spending time abroad is that it gives you the chance to experience different cultures, and there are two sides to this. One is the need to fit in with national and local ideas of behaviour. As in the UK, there can be differences culturally between urban and rural areas in the same country. The other is the viewpoint that wants to export a sense of Britishness wherever you go. This might be acceptable, but it's important to be sensitive to local perceptions. For example, the Ibiza clubber stereotype might be fine in parts of that island, but not OK elsewhere.

Wherever possible, it's worth doing some research about local culture before you go.

Case study
Social life
Learning to live in France took some time to get used to, the social life being very different to young British culture. Although the French are very stylish throughout the day, when going out to bars/clubs they don't tend to dress up as we British do. They also don't tend to drink so much in a small space of time.

Drugs

Although a few countries, notably the Netherlands, have high-profile, liberal soft drugs laws, in most countries drug use is likely to be illegal. The best advice is to avoid it – in some areas of the world the penalties for possession are very severe.

E111
(See 'Health'.)

E128
This form provides health cover and treatment, and replaces the E111 form for students studying in another EEA country. A considerable benefit is that it covers you for treatment for any condition for the duration of your course. However, there are a number of restrictions relating to the period of study abroad, the type of course and whether the course is compulsory or voluntary. The E128 has a limited time span of two years although this can be only for 12 months in certain circumstances. Apply to:

The Inland Revenue
National Insurance Contributions Office
International Services
Longbenton
Newcastle-upon-Tyne NE98 1ZZ
Tel: 0845 915 4811

The Department of Health website, www.doh.gov.uk, also has some useful information.

Erasmus scheme
Erasmus is the scheme that promotes student mobility and exchanges within most of Europe – the 24 EU countries (Austria, Belgium, Cyprus, the Czech Republic, Denmark, Estonia, Finland, France, Germany, Greece, Hungary, Ireland, Italy, Latvia, Lithuania, Luxembourg, Malta, the Netherlands, Poland, Portugal, Slovakia, Slovenia, Spain, Sweden and the UK), the EEA countries (Iceland, Liechtenstein and Norway) and two other partners (Bulgaria and Romania). More than 100,000 students take part every year, with about 10 per cent coming from the UK.

The key point about Erasmus is that it gives you the chance to study for your degree in another country and, through the European Credit Transfer Scheme (ECTS – see below), receive full credit for the work that you do abroad from your home institution.

The main features of the scheme are as follows:

- study periods abroad last for a minimum of three months and a maximum of 12
- you can't join the scheme during your first year of higher education study

- if you study abroad with Erasmus for a full year, you pay no tuition fees to your home university
- work experience for some schemes can be arranged by your host university
- some UK courses, such as language degrees, offer the whole third year of a four-year degree in another European university within the Erasmus scheme.

The links between universities within the Erasmus scheme are organised by the individual institutions. Most universities and colleges will have someone who is responsible for organising the Erasmus work, and you should contact them to discover the opportunities that are available through your home institution.

European Credit Transfer Scheme (ECTS)

ECTS is a scheme funded by the European Commission that attempts to work out equivalences of qualification in higher education courses across Europe. This means that, in theory, a course (or part of a course) that's taken in one country can be credited towards a qualification in another. Normally, this is the basis under which any Erasmus/Socrates exchange takes place, but you should confirm this with the university concerned.

(For countries outside the ECTS scheme, see 'Qualifications'.)

Gay and lesbian

(See 'Lifestyle'.)

Health

See the booklet *Health for Travellers Abroad* that's supplied with the E111 form (see 'Insurance'). This gives you all the information you need on topics such as essential vaccinations, food and details of areas where the water supply might be unreliable.

It's also worth keeping an eye on new health scares that can affect particular countries around the world, such as the SARS outbreak that restricted travel to parts of Canada and China in 2003. If you have any concerns, it's a good idea to check out the travel advisories issued by the government. These can be found at the Foreign Office website (www.fco.gov.org), or you can call their helpline (Tel: 0870 606 0290).

How to apply

In most cases, in order to apply for exchange programmes you should contact your own university's international office (or the international coordinator in your own faculty). If there is no exchange to a location that you want, it may be worth approaching the international office at the overseas institution in which you're interested. Formal exchange programmes can take some time to get established, though.

In the country directory you'll find details of application procedures for undertaking non-exchange, full-time study overseas. Application procedures change very significantly from one country to another.

Insurance

This isn't something that you've bothered about so far, but it will be a vital part of preparation for your travels.

For health purposes, as a minimum you need to get hold of form E111 from your local social services department or post office. This enables you to reclaim some of the costs of medical treatment if you become ill when you're away in EU countries. In addition, the UK has reciprocal arrangements with around 60 countries worldwide (but many aren't covered – details are given in the booklet supplied to you with the form).

You need to fill in your personal details (giving basic information such as your national insurance (NI) number). The key points about E111 cover are that it only covers *some* of the costs, and that you recover the costs. This means that you have to pay in advance for any treatment and (although we hope you don't have to use it), you need to allow for this in your budget. Remember also that you probably won't get all the money back, and that health costs abroad can be very high.

The best way to cover yourself is to take out medical insurance. Most insurance companies have holiday insurance schemes that can be extended to cover longer periods abroad. However, costs go up according to the time that you spend away and the areas that you're visiting. It's worth doing some shopping around before you go to get the best deal, but any policy should cover areas such as getting you back home to the UK in the event of serious illness or even death.

You should also take out insurance cover for your personal possessions.

Languages

Unless you're planning to study in Australia, Ireland, South Africa or the US, you may well have to learn a foreign language. Even in countries such as the Scandinavian ones, where teaching programmes are in English, it's possible that you might have to present work in the host language. The chance to learn is a positive opportunity which can benefit you in many ways.

Case study

Learning languages – 3

One major piece of advice would be that you don't live with fellow English-speaking students, as I did. Of course it was reassuring having them around but it definitely stunts the language learning curve. In my first year I lived with an English and an Irish guy, and although it was great fun living with them it made us lazy when it came to speaking French. The turning point for me was moving to Paris for six months and being constantly surrounded by French-speaking people. My French improved considerably at that stage.

Lifestyle

Attitudes towards different lifestyles vary from country to country, as well as within countries. As a general rule, capital cities and urban areas tend to be more accepting of alternative living than smaller towns and more rural areas. You'll find some basic guidance under the individual country entries in this guide, but it's best to do some research and get local views before you travel.

Case study

Meeting other students

During my study period in Pamplona I had the chance to meet loads of people from many different countries, cultures and backgrounds and share with them a unique experience, which I realise I will never be able to repeat in my life.

Living costs abroad

Costs abroad can vary according to exchange rate fluctuations. The main issue is likely to be whether it's going to cost you more to live abroad than it would do in the UK. One of the neatest ways of estimating this is what's known as the 'Big Mac Index'. This is produced on a regular basis by the *Economist* and gives the price of a Big Mac in various countries around the world. (You can check out regular updates at the *Economist* website: www.economist.com.)

Of course, this is only a rough estimate of living costs, but it does give some idea of comparative costs. The best way to live as cheaply as possible abroad is to find out where the locals go to eat and shop. In many places, open-air markets are the best and cheapest places to buy food, even though there may be many things on sale that are unfamiliar (you might also find yourself bemused by the range of choice on offer).

Permits and visas

British citizens who hold a full British passport can stay or work in any country in the EU/EEA for up to three months without a visa or work permit. If you want to stay longer you'll need to get a resident's permit, although this is usually a pretty straightforward process.

You must check at the outset with the embassy or the consulate of the country in which you intend to stay, as the procedure to get a permit before you leave the UK differs from country to country.

For countries outside of the EU and the EEA, it's very important that you check whether visas are required for your stay – for most countries you'll need to get a visa before you leave the UK. (This guide gives visa and permit information as known at the time of writing under the individual country entries.)

Qualifications (comparability with British qualifications)

Outside of the ECTS scheme, understanding how a course and qualification in one country compares with the same in another country is a bit more difficult.

In many countries, bachelor degrees take four years. Because of this, many countries regard their courses as rather higher in academic terms than the UK. The actual comparability of courses in exchanges outside of the area covered by ECTS is often decided between institutions working within guidelines. If you are thinking about an exchange of this type, you need to discuss this issue in detail with your home institution.

But if you are one of the increasing number of UK students who are thinking about doing a complete undergraduate degree abroad, there is another range of issues to consider.

First, if you are planning to work in a specific career or profession, you need to check that the qualification that you'll receive from the overseas institution is accepted in the UK (or any other country in which you plan to work). For some professions (law, veterinary, medicine, etc) there is some recognition from one country to another, but this isn't generally the case. Your first port of call for more information is likely to be the body governing the profession that you're interested in (such as the Law Society).

For more general enquiries about equivalence of qualifications, the UK body that provides advice is the National Academic Recognition Information Centre (NARIC – see Useful Addresses and Publications).

Religion

The issue of religion is important. If you're active in your church environment, it's worth checking whether the same form of worship will be possible where you intend to go. The Anglican Church has networks in many parts of the world, some of them in surprising locations too. There is also the religious view on alcohol to consider (for example, Moslem countries tend to be teetotal), and this is worth checking also.

Safe and unsafe places

Global, regional and even local politics mean that some places are safe to visit, and others are very much to be avoided. If you have any doubts, check out the Foreign Office's travel advice (www.fco.gov.org; helpline: 0870 606 0290).

The government divides the safety of countries into three areas:

1. significant risk
2. high risk, and
3. extreme risk: do not travel to any part of the country.

In May 2003, the *Daily Telegraph* brought together travel advice from the governments in Australia, Germany, New Zealand, the UK and USA.

These combined warnings can be found in the box below.

Threats worldwide

1 – Areas of significant risk	*2 – Areas of high risk*	*3 – Areas of extreme risk (do not travel to any part of the country)*
Angola	Albania	Afghanistan
Brunei	Azerbaijan	Algeria
China (Xin Jiang province)	Chad	Burundi
Djibouti	Colombia	Caucasus
Egypt	Congo	Central African
Eritrea	East Timor	Republic
Haiti	Ecuador	Chechen Republic
Iran	Ethiopia	Dagestan
Kosovo	Georgia	Democratic
Kuwait	Guinea	Republic of Congo
Libya	Indonesia	Iraq
Malaysia	Iran	Ivory Coast
Morocco	Israel	Jammu and
Namibia	Jordan	Kashmir
Nigeria	Kenya	Liberia
Oman	Kyrgyzstan	Yemen
Pakistan	Lebanon	
Papua New Guinea	Nepal	
Quatar	Philippines	
Rwanda	Saudi Arabia	
Sierra Leone	Somalia	
Singapore	Sudan	
Solomon Islands	Syria	
Sri Lanka	Tanzania	
Tajikstan	Uzbekistan	
Thailand		
Tunisia		
United Arab Emirates		

Teaching and learning methods

These could be different to the styles of teaching and learning that you've become used to in the UK, whether more or less formal. There can be a very different approach to your tutors, for example, in many countries you won't be assigned a personal tutor. In some countries the relationship between tutors and students is more structured than it is in the UK (although perhaps this is changing).

Case study

Teaching styles – 2

The approach of the department that I was visiting was somewhat impersonal and distant compared to my home department in Manchester. The lectures were very large and there was very little one-to-one or few-to-one contact with academic staff. Lectures were primarily about copying down verbatim what the lecturer wrote on the board, with precious little opportunity for interruptions or friendly banter. My tutor in Manchester, also a professor, would make sure to take us out for a pub lunch at least once a term.

In some areas, students might not have the same privileges that they expect in the UK. In Spain, for example, there are universities where undergraduates have no access to the library for working, only to borrow books.

Travelling

Clearly, you'll be looking at travel to and from your chosen area of study in some depth before you go (don't forget the possible need to return quickly in the event of a crisis).

Currently, many air fares around Europe are at their cheapest levels ever. But they can get very booked up during key periods of the year, such as Christmas, so you'll probably have to plan well in advance, and be prepared to pay premium rates to get a ticket home.

Eurostar has opened up direct access to European train services. At best, they're excellent and often much cheaper than in the UK. This isn't a universal truth though, as trains in Europe don't always run on time and can be expensive. For many of these special services, booking is recommended well in advance.

Outside of Europe, the position is much less clear. Although the specialist travel pages of daily newspapers carry headline rates showing very cheap fares, these are often limited to return travel within specified periods, and these may well not suit your needs. What you can do is to discuss your travel plans with one of the student-orientated travel services.

Visas

(See Permits and visas.)

When to apply

This varies from country to country (you can find some details in the country entries in this guide). Potential exchange students should consult their home institution. The key message is to be well prepared, and apply as early as you can.

Case study

The real experience – 2

Going abroad is a very valuable experience and something I feel everyone should consider. The exchange allowed me to gain a lot of confidence and I now feel very at ease with the prospect of eventually leaving the UK and working abroad on my own. I would definitely do it again and recommend it to anyone whatever their age or background.

Directory of Countries

Country profile: Australia

Population

18.5 million. The main city, Sydney, has a population of 3.7 million.

History/government

Australia was the last great land mass to be colonised by Europeans in the late 18th and 19th centuries. But Australian history goes back some 50,000 years. Although Australia's modern history has been shaped by close colonial ties with the UK and its past as a penal colony, the presence of some 230,000 Aborigines, mostly living in the northern and central areas, shows a different picture.

Australia's parliamentary system is similar to the UK: the Crown is represented by the governor-general. Although Australia is fully independent, there are ongoing debates about becoming a republic.

Culture, language and lifestyle

Outdoor lifestyle, culture and sporting success (in cricket, rugby, and Australian Rules football) is central to Australian identity, and the country still has close ties with the UK. There is no particular Australian cuisine, but the barbecue is a main social event. Australians have a close connection with nature – backpacking, trekking and travel to the Outback are very popular.

The lifestyle varies from area to area. The major cities can be vibrant and lively places but other areas can seem very quiet. The long distances between towns can present a problem when travelling around.

Banking system/currency

The Australian dollar (A$). Bank opening hours are from 8.30am–4.30pm, Monday to Friday; ATMs are available everywhere, especially in major cities.

Climate/geography

Australia has three time zones, and some variations of climate. Most cities are warm and temperate. The central area is hot desert and the northern territories are humid and tropical. There is a real contrast between the urban populated areas and the Outback, where distances are vast, drought is frequent and settlements are scattered and sparse.

Transport
Most international airlines fly to Sydney, Melbourne, Brisbane and Perth. Flying is best for internal travel, if quite expensive. Long-distance train and bus services are cheaper, but time-consuming.

Health arrangements
You will need to pass a medical examination and obtain Overseas Student Health Cover (OSHC). Your home university can advise you about policies existing for exchange students at competitive rates. Without proof of medical cover you won't be issued with a visa – it's best to consult the Australian Consulate about this.

Higher education
There are 53 universities, as well as a number of private institutions. The bachelor's degree normally takes three years to complete, although professional subjects such as medicine take six years.

History of accepting foreign students
In recent years, Australia has developed as a centre for international study, both for full-time students and those on exchanges or scholar-ships; it has especially strong connections with Asia. There is a well-structured system, through international offices, to deal with all aspects of the process.

Fees
For full-time study, fees range from A$1,200 to A$27,000 a year, depending on the course and institution. You'll need to think carefully about finance before applying. A small number of scholarships for study and research may be available from the Association of Commonwealth Universities (ACU). For exchanges, check with your home university's international office to find out whether fee-waiving exists.

Working while studying
If you have a student visa, you can work 20 hours a week. However, you must have a main source of income, or your application won't be accepted by the Australian government.

Application system/visas
You need to apply for a study visa from the Australian Consulate – in order to get this you must pay a non-refundable fee, have a medical examination and be accepted on a registered course as a full-time or exchange student. You also need evidence of medical insurance for your stay. You must be issued with an OAF (overseas acceptance form) by the ACU; the Australian High Commission provides useful information about visa procedures.

Expenses/costs
In addition to any fees, budget for about A$320 per week on accommodation and basic living expenses (allow for more in cities such as Melbourne and Sydney).

Accommodation/assistance
Almost all Australian universities have housing or accommodation services available, whether in halls of residence or private.

Academic year
This is divided into two semesters: semester 1 typically runs from March–June, and semester 2 from July–November.

Support network
Usually very good, ranging from assistance with accommodation, welfare and health matters to clubs and societies specifically for international students. The main point of contact is the university international office.

Volume/type of work
This depends on your subject – Australian universities have strong links with the UK, although the grading system is similar to the USA. The workload usually consists of coursework, examinations and projects. Whatever your discipline, take the opportunity to do an option in Australian studies; as an exchange student, this may be part of your programme.

Useful addresses/websites
Australia High Commission
Australia House
Strand
London WC2B 4LA
Tel: 020 7379 4334
Fax: 020 7240 5333
Website: www.australia.org.uk

Australian Consulate
First Floor, Century House
11 St Peter's Square
Manchester M2 3DJ
Tel: 0161 273 9440
Fax: 0161 237 9135

Association of Commonwealth Universities (ACU)
36 Gordon Square
London WC1H OPF

Tel: 020 7380 6700
Fax: 020 7367 2655
Email: info@acu.uk
Website: www.acu.ac.ukn

Case study 1
Monash University
(Incorporating Monash International), Melbourne

Background
Established in 1961, Monash has grown into a dynamic, multicultural institution, with six campuses in or around Melbourne. It also has two overseas campuses in Malaysia and South Africa, and centres in Milan and London. Melbourne is a cosmopolitan city, considered to be the most European in Australia.

Structure
Monash has over 44,000 students from over 100 countries, of which some 9,000 study through Monash International. Internationalism is a key aspect of the curriculum. A full range of academic subjects is on offer.

Social life
There's an extensive student support system with excellent entertainment and recreational facilities on campus. Melbourne has many pubs, bars and restaurants reflecting the city's ethnic diversity. The Victoria Market is a legacy of Melbourne's past, and the area along the Yarra River is a cultural centre with theatres, galleries and museums. If you like sport, the MCG is a magnificent stadium for cricket and Australian Rules football. An attractive and lively place to study.

Applications/accommodation
Full-time students should enrol at least two months prior to the course commencement date – aim to arrive in Melbourne for induction and orientation 14 days in advance of the programme start. Check the admissions link on the Monash International website for full details on application procedure and fees. Accommodation options are campus halls, homestay (full/part board), hostels or rented accommodation. All international students receive a copy of the accommodation guide, and housing officers will help. The university suggests that students budget for between A$17,800 and A$19,150 a year in total living costs.

Exchange students should contact their home institution's international office to see whether bilateral links exist with Monash.

Contact
Monash University International Centre
Monash International University
Building 73
Clayton
Victoria 3800
Australia
Tel: (+61) 392 674852
Fax: (+61) 396 274862
Email: study@monash.edu.au
Website: www.monash.edu.au

Case study 2
University of Southern Queensland (USQ), Toowoomba, Queensland

Background
USQ was founded in 1967, and is located on a spacious campus about 10 minutes' drive from the small city of Toowoomba (two hours away from Brisbane). It has a population of 90,000 and has been voted the best city to live in Australia.

Structure
USQ has six faculties, from arts to education and science, emphasising a strong professional and vocational aspect as well as academic proficiency. There are around 5,000 students on campus, of which some 600 are international students from over 40 countries. Studying at USQ is small scale, friendly, informal and supportive.

Social life
Revolves around the campus, as bus services to Toowoomba itself are infrequent in the evening (you really need access to a car). Campus life is lively, with many social and recreational activities. Queensland has the Gold Coast and the semi-tropical north as highlights – outdoor living is the centre of student experience here.

Applications/accommodation

Information relating to admissions can be found by clicking on the appropriate link on the USQ website. Costs are lower – budget for about A$8,000 per year to cover basic living costs. Accommodation options are available on campus and in Toowoomba (less convenient, but cheaper). The international office at USQ is very helpful.

Contact

University of Southern Queensland International
Toowoomba
Queensland 4350
Australia
Tel: (+61) 746 312362
Fax: (+61) 746 362211
Email: international@usq.edu.au
Website: www.usq.edu.au/international/

Country profile: Austria

Population
8 million. The capital, Vienna, has a population of 1.66 million.

History/government
Given its geographical location at the heart of Europe, and its strategic position, Austria is a key player in international politics. It's a federal republic and became an EU Member State in 1992.

Culture, language and lifestyle
The language is Austrian German. Cities such as Vienna and Salzburg are important as cultural centres, and Austria is often called 'The Land of Music', its celebrated composers ranging from Mozart to Strauss. Outdoor life is popular, with activities including skiing, mountain biking, hiking and paragliding. Traditional Austrian cuisine consists of many meat and vegetable dishes, sauerkraut, followed by pastries and rich desserts, often washed down by excellent beer.

Vienna has a sense of faded imperial glory as well as being the cultural capital for 'Mitteleuropa', and regional centres have a similar feel. Austria has a high standard of living and a strong café culture.

Banking system/currency
The euro (€). Banks are open from Monday–Friday, 7.45am–12.30pm and 2.15–4pm. Before opening a bank account, ask about special free student packages (there is an age limit of 26 for this). Post offices also offer banking services.

Climate/geography
Austria has a temperate continental climate: cold winters with frequent rains in the lowland regions and snow in the mountains, and cool summers. It's a very picturesque country, as the Alpine range covers two-thirds of the country.

Transport
There is a major international airport at Vienna and smaller airports in Salzburg and Innsbruck. The transport system in Austria is highly developed and generally very efficient. Trains are comfortable, clean and reasonably frequent.

Health arrangements
If you are resident in the UK you should take with you a completed E111 or E128 for a longer stay in the country, which entitles you to emergency medical treatment on the same terms as Austrian nationals. However, this isn't a substitute for full travel insurance.

Higher education

In recent years there have been significant changes in the Austrian higher education system. There are 19 state universities, including the University of Vienna (with 66,000 students, making it one of the largest in Europe). These offer the complete range of academic disciplines, although some of the newer ones, such as Linz, provide a smaller number of subjects.

Fachhochschulen offer university-level courses with a more practical/vocational orientation. There are also a number of private institutions and several specialist/technical universities. Whether you're considering full-time study or an exchange, think carefully about which type of institution will best suit your interests. A bachelor's degree takes 3–4 years to complete.

History of accepting foreign students

The most common way for students from the UK to study in Austria is through an exchange programme. Your home university's international office can tell you whether and where bilateral links have been set up – there are many of these between Austrian and UK institutions.

UK nationals can study full-time courses in Austria and be treated in the same way as Austrian nationals – all teaching takes place in German, so thorough knowledge of the language is essential. Students must demonstrate evidence of their competence in German, or will have to take the *Hochschulsprachprüfung* (German proficiency examination). If you're an exchange student it is possible to follow some options in English, but be sure to check this in advance of going on the exchange.

Fees

In October 2001 the Austrian government introduced tuition fees ranging between €363.36 and €726.72 a year, depending on the institution and programme of study. You should check with the institution to which you are applying.

Working while studying

It's sometimes possible to find part-time work to supplement your income, particularly in major cities or via the tourist sector (for example, skiing). However, you'll need good knowledge of German to do this.

Application/visa system

Nationals of EU/EEA do not need a visa. Within three working days of entry to Austria, you have to register with the municipal authorities (*Magistratisches Bezirksamt* in Vienna; *Magistrat* or *Gemeindeamt* in the other university locations). Registration forms (*Meldezettel*) are available there; if you're staying at a guesthouse or a hotel, the landlord/landlady or the management will take care of the registration.

Exchange students should contact their home international office initially. Full-time students make their applications direct to each university. Application forms and details of admission procedures are available from the *Studienabteilung* (university director's office) at each institution.

Some courses recruit during the winter semester and some during the summer, and you are advised to apply as early as possible. The deadline for applications for the winter semester is 1 September and for the summer semester, 1 February. Information about studying in Austria is available from the Austrian Foreign Student Service (ÖAD).

Expenses/costs

Major cities such as Vienna can be expensive, particularly for accommodation. Budget for €765 monthly to cover general living costs – accommodation is approximately €290 a month. These are general guidelines and will vary depending on location and lifestyle.

Accommodation/assistance

Generally, students are expected to find their own accommodation. The Austrian National Union of Students (ÖH, *Österreichische Hochschülerschaft*) offers a housing information service in each university. ÖAD can provide accommodation for exchange students and those receiving scholarships from the Austrian government. There are a number of fairly cheap hotels and boarding houses in most towns, as well as hostels. Renting a room or an apartment in the private market is very difficult and expensive. Information on this type of accommodation is available from the Student Union and local newspapers.

Academic year

This is divided into two semesters, running from October–June.

Support network

The ÖH has a number of sections that promote activities such as sport and entertainment. The union also operates subsidised restaurants and cafeterias. Some universities have a 'buddy system', where students with previous international experience offer a helping hand to new students.

Volume/type of work

Courses are generally taught through a mixture of lectures, seminars and presentations, followed by an exam. Much depends on the type of course followed – there are more practical units, together with project-based assessment and exercises in *Fachhochschülen* courses.

Useful addresses/websites

Austrian Cultural Forum

28 Rutland Gate
London SW7 1PQ
Tel: 020 7584 8853
Fax: 020 7225 0470
Email: culture@austria.org.uk
Website: www.austria.org.uk/culture/

Austrian Embassy
19 Belgrave Mews West
London SW1X 8HU
Tel: 020 7235 3731
Fax: 020 7344 0292
Email: embassy@austria.org.uk
Website: www.austria.org.uk

Austrian Foreign Student Service (ÖAD)
Alserstrasse 4/1/15/7
1090 Vienna
Austria
Email: lydia.skarits@oead.ac.at

Federal Ministry of Education
Minoritenplatz 5
A-1014 Vienna
Austria
Tel: (+43) 01 531 200
Fax: (+43) 01 531 28099
Email: ministerium@brnbwk.gv.at
Website: www.bmwk.gv.at

Österreichische Hochschülerschaft (ÖH)
Liechensteinstrasse 13/15
A-1090 Vienna
Austria
Tel: (+43) 01 310 88800
Website: www.oeh.ac.at/

Case study 1
Universität Innsbruck (University of Innsbruck)

Background
This is western Austria's largest institution of higher education,
and one of Austria's oldest universities, dating back to 1562.

Structure

A public university with tuition fees – free tuition is granted to those studying within international mobility programme. The university has four faculties and 23,000 students. Since teaching is in German (almost without exception), fluency is a prerequisite to attending lectures and passing examinations. A full list of studies can be found at: www.uibk.ac.at/C101/Studienabteilung (click on *Studien-möglichkeiten*).

Social life

The city has developed an interesting social scene in recent years. There are a number of cultural associations, theatre groups and many student bars and cafes. In the Ing-Etzel-Strasse, several bars stay open till 4am.

Applications/accommodation

The Austrian Academic Exchange Service (ÖAD) will do its best to organise a room for you, although a limited number are available (email for an application form at: oead-housing@uibk.ac.at). Exchange students have priority, and a deposit of €400 is payable. Double and single rooms are available, with kitchens and bathrooms usually shared. Rooms are allocated in order of arrival of both application and deposit. Renting a room or apartment in the private market is difficult and expensive: one room apartments are estimated at between €327 and €400 a month. The student union homepage (www.oehinfo.uibk.ac.at) gives you more information on this type of accommodation.

Applications for full-time study should be made directly to the university by February of the intended year of study. Exchange students should apply via the international office of their home institution.

Contact

Universität Innsbruck
Innrain 52
A-6020 Innsbruck
Austria
Tel: (+43) 512 5070
Fax: (+43) 507 2800
Email: admin@uibk.ac.at
Website: www.uibk.ac.at

Case study 2
Fachhochschüle, Salzburg (FH Salzburg)

Background
During recent decades Salzburg has developed as a cultural centre, above all as the city of Mozart – from festivals attracting tourists from all over the world, to its winter focus as a ski centre. Salzburg is compact, architecturally beautiful and cosmopolitan.

Structure
Founded in 1994 and close to the city centre, FH Salzburg offers vocational and professional degree-level courses, and five degree programmes (telecommunications engineering, multimedia art, business and information management, digital TV and interactive services), and a part-time programme (business development in tourism). It's an innovative, small and friendly place to study, with fewer than 2,000 full-time students.

The school has expanded its international links and now has several bilateral agreements with UK institutions. Part of this process is to increase the number of programmes offered in English, but knowledge of German is still important and allows for more study options. Your international office can give you information on availability of courses in English. Full-time students have to pay fees (approx €500 per semester), full details can be obtained from the international office.

Social life
Salzburg has many cafes, bars and restaurants in the heart of the old town (Mozartplatz). There are museums, churches, castles and galleries to discover, all steeped in history. You're within easy reach of the mountains and some great scenery – and there are good rail connections to Munich and Vienna. A charming and distinctive place to live and study.

Applications/accommodation
FH Salzburg has different admission procedures for its study programmes. Basic requirement is the general university entrance qualification (secondary school leaving certificate). Exchange students must be part of a bilateral agreement, and full-time applicants must show a sufficient command of German.

FH Salzburg international office is friendly and helpful, it's your first point of call for accommodation queries – be sure to contact them well in advance. Apartments in the centre of Salzburg can be quite expensive and difficult to find – the FH offers affordable accommodation in either halls with other international students, or in private houses. Cost varies depending on facilities and location, but budget for €300–350 for accommodation monthly, with another €400–450 monthly for other basic living costs.

Contact
Fachhochschüle Salzburg
Schillerstrasse 30
A-5020 Salzburg
Austria
Tel: (+43) 662 466 5623
Fax: (+43) 662 446 5559
Email: admin@fh-sbg.ac.at
Website: www.fh-sbg.ac.at

Country profile: Belgium

Population
10 million. The capital, Brussels, has a population of 1m.

History/government
The ideal location at the centre of Europe – the headquarters of the EU as well as NATO. Belgium was a founder member of the EEC in 1957.

Culture, language and lifestyle
Belgium is culturally divided into French-speaking (31 per cent) and Flemish (58 per cent). Each area has its own cultural character, but Brussels is difficult to pin down, as it's multicultural. English is spoken widely in the French area, but less so in the Flemish region. Belgium's cuisine is highly regarded – eating out isn't cheap, but it is high quality. There's an amazing range of beers.

Although some 75 per cent of Belgians are said to be Catholic, many do not now participate. There is excellent eating and drinking, and other activities such as clubbing are enthusiastic and relatively cheap, if not cutting edge.

Banking system/currency
The euro (€). Bank opening hours run from 9am–4pm, and ATMs are widely available.

Climate/geography
Three areas make up the country: a flat coastal plain, the central plateau and the mountainous Ardennes. Generally, Belgium experiences mild summers, cool winters, and it can be rainy and humid.

Transport
There is an extensive motorway and rail network.

Health arrangements
Take an E111 with you to use, but be sure that your status is made clear as a non-private patient before you have treatment or a consultation. It's best to take out health insurance cover.

Higher education
Only six institutions offer full degree programmes. Teaching is in either French or German, according to the region. Higher education works in three cycles: the first is generalised study (2–3 years); the second, more specialised (leading to the *Licencaat*); the third leads to a doctorate.

History of accepting foreign students
You'll need a working knowledge of either French, German or Flemish, depending on where you're studying, and you may have to take a language test. There are some restrictions on numbers of foreign students set by individual institutions.

Fees
These are set by individual institutions.

Working while studying
This should be possible as EU employment rules apply in Belgium.

Application system/visas
For this, you apply direct to the institution – each has its own procedures and closing dates. Visas are not required for EU nationals.

Expenses/costs
It's best to budget for more than €600 monthly for food, transport, health insurance and accommodation (around €270 should be set aside for monthly rent).

Accommodation/assistance
Most higher education institutions have a social service system, and it should be reasonably easy to find housing either in halls or rooms.

Support network
Student Union services are extensive. Some institutions also have an expatriate society.

Volume/type of work
This tends to be quite heavy – there are fairly formal teaching programmes and exam assessment.

Useful addresses/websites
Belgian Embassy
103–5 Eaton Square
London SW1W 9AB
Tel: 020 7470 3700
Fax: 020 7259 6213
Email: info@belgium-embassy.co.uk
Website: www.belgium-embassy.co.uk

Ministry of Education (Flemish speaking)
Henri Consciencegebow
Konig Albert II Laan 15
1210 Brussels

Belgium
Tel: (+32) 2 553 8611

Ministry of Education (French speaking)
Rue Royal 204
1010 Brussels
Belgium
Tel: (+32) 2 210 5511

Case study
Université Libre de Bruxelles (ULB)
(Free University of Brussels)

Background
Founded in 1834, it is now one of the best-known French-speaking universities in the world with over 18,000 students. Brussels is the hub of life in Belgium and has a very lively scene. Its Grand Place is stunning – probably the best-preserved square in Europe. The university has a very positive attitude to student mobility around Europe, as it participates in the Erasmus/Socrates scheme.

Structure
The university has 18 faculties and schools, as well as several hospitals based in three campuses in Brussels, and four across the Wallonia region. The department and faculty secretariats play an important role, both as information sources and in the practical aspects of studying. ULB has a facility to provide printed versions of lecture notes, legal advice centre, medical centre and childcare facilities.

Social life
Brussels has some very lively clubs and bars, but can seem a bit quiet at weekends (when many of the workers at EU institutions go home). Although these activities are reasonably priced, eating out can be expensive. There is an active student scene and the Student Union has programmes of activities. ULB has its own campus radio, the sports centre organises more than 50 sports and there are also facilities for music, dance, painting, theatre, etc.

Applications/accommodation
For exchanges, contact your home institution – ULB's international relations department administers the scheme. For full-time study, contact the registration and admissions department for details, as you will need to present documentation, depending on

the study programme you wish to take. The department will also provide details of any tuition fees.

For accommodation, apply to the accommodation office for a campus room – prices vary according to style and comfort. The office can also supply a list of private lettings (before 15 June).

Contact
Cellule info-études
Université Libre de Bruxelles
Avenue Bayl 87a
B-1050 Bruxelles
Belgium
Tel: (+32) 02 650 36 36
Website: www.ulb.ac.be/

Country profile: Canada

Population
30.4 million. Its capital, Ottawa, has a population of 1 million.

History/government
The country became self-governing in 1867, although Canada later became a member of the Commonwealth. It's a constitutional monarchy (the Queen is the formal head of state) and a federal democracy. Its official languages are English and French. Canada's main political issue continues to be the relationship between the French-speaking province of Quebec and the rest of the country.

Culture, language and lifestyle
Canada's Native Canadian, French and British traditions give the country a complex three-dimensional character. Add to this more recent changes, making modern Canada's society widely multicultural. Art, music and literature reflect this diversity; there's a fascinating contrast between metropolitan life and the barren wilderness of the far north, where people still live a nomadic lifestyle based around hunting and trapping. Canadian cuisine reflects this diversity. Seafood is plentiful and cheap, and dairy products are good. Quebec has its own distinctive menu.

Canada is diverse and the lifestyle is heavily influenced by the US, with the notable exception of Quebec which is very European.

Banking system/currency
The Canadian dollar (CAN$). Bank opening times are Monday–Friday, from 9am–5pm.

Climate/geography
Wide variations, from the permanently frozen ice caps of the far north to the lush vegetation of British Columbia. Winters are cold, and you can expect a lot of snow (even in the cities), although summers can be hot and humid at times.

Canada is a mountainous country; the spectacular Rockies are a dramatic feature. There are also many lakes and rivers in the unspoilt wilderness or the national parks.

Transport
Internal flights tend to be expensive but sometimes the only viable way to travel, due to the distances involved. If you don't mind taking the time, travel via bus (especially Canadian Greyhound) is much cheaper and more interesting. Train services are limited, but it can be a captivating way of seeing the landscape.

Health arrangements

To secure even basic medical care in Canada you need to take out comprehensive medical insurance.

Higher education

There are 83 universities in Canada, along with a number of community colleges and private institutions: these are run under the authority of the provincial/territorial governments. Each university sets their own admission requirements. The system (apart from Quebec) reflects a combination of British and American educational philosophies – a bachelor's degree lasts between 3 and 4 years, and tends to be more general in nature than a typical UK degree. It is common practice to major in one subject, and take a number of other general subjects to make up the degree.

History of accepting foreign students

All universities accept international students, and many have developed programmes with overseas partners (including some with strong UK links). All teaching is in English (unless you choose to study in Quebec). Links are usually well organised, with the international office being the focal point for support and assistance.

Fees

Canadian universities are fee-paying. The average cost for a foreign student for one school year (8 months) in an arts and science programme is CAN$7,100. Tuition costs vary from institution to institution, ranging from CAN$5,000 to CAN$10,000 for undergraduate courses.

In Quebec, fees are set by the Ministry of Education. Foreign students have to pay a base fee and supplementary fees. In addition to tuition fees, other fees may apply. Some foreign students may be entitled to an exemption under the terms of international agreements and should apply for this at their embassies.

Working while studying

Full-time students are allowed to work on campus without the need for a work permit. You can also find part-time employment to boost your income, especially in the service industries in the major cities. However, you'll need a temporary work permit for this (details are available from the Canadian High Commission).

Application system/visas

Each university sets its own admission standards and assesses the qualifications of each applicant individually. An international student, you can take a degree either at an English-language or French-language institution, but you don't have to be fluent in both languages to go to a Canadian university.

Visas are required if you intend to study for longer than six months – otherwise they are not required for UK students. Students from other European countries should check their status with the Canadian High Commission.

If you're a European student and planning to study in Quebec, you must get a Certificat d'acceptation du Gouvernement du Québec (Quebec Government Certificate of Acceptance) and a student visa. Once the institution has accepted you, you need to contact the Quebec authorities and Canadian diplomatic mission for the region where you plan to study, showing proof that you've been accepted to the university full-time, and that you have the necessary finance.

These authorisations have to be obtained before you get to Canada, and are only given to full-time students.

Expenses/costs

Canada has a higher standard of living than the UK, but at a lower cost on the whole. Typical living costs for the eight-month academic year are around CAN$8,000, with accommodation accounting for as much as half of this. In Quebec, the law requires foreign students to get health insurance that is valid there. The annual cost of coverage is added to the tuition bill (cost for the 2002–3 academic year was CAN$588). This insurance plan covers medical and hospital costs, along with prescription medicines. It does not cover dental care or glasses. There is also coverage for repatriation in case of death or disability.

Accommodation/assistance

There are numerous options – much depends on location and lifestyle, with Toronto and Montreal being more expensive than smaller towns and cities. Halls are one option, private rented apartments or shared student houses another.

Academic year

The university year usually runs from September–May. Some universities are on a semester or trimester system, with all courses available even in the summer.

Support network

Canada is a country of immigrants and has both a tradition and policy of encouraging multicultural diversity. Most universities have Student Unions and a wide range of campus support systems.

Volume/type of work

This will depend on your subject, but you can expect to go to a range of lectures, tutorials and workshops, focusing primarily on your major subject. Assessment is usually through coursework, examination and projects, backed up by a lot of independent study.

Useful addresses/websites
Association of Commonwealth Universities (ACU)
John Foster House
36 Gordon Square
London WC1H ODF
Tel: 020 7380 6700
Fax: 020 7367 2655
Email: info@acc.uk
Website: www.acu.ac.uk

Association of Universities and Colleges of Canada
Suite 600
350 Albert Street
Ottawa
Ontario K1R 1B1
Canada
Tel: (+1) 613 563 1236
Fax: (+1) 613 563 9475
Email: info@aucc.ca
Website: www.aucc.ca

Canadian High Commission
38 Grosvenor Square
London W1X 4AA
Tel: 020 7258 8600
Fax: 020 7258 8506
Website: www.canada.org.uk

Service d'Immigration de Québec
Delegation Générale du Québec
87–88 Rue la Boetie
75008 Paris
France
Tel: (+33) 01 53 93 45 45
Fax: (+33) 01 53 93 45 40
Website: www.immg.gouv.qc.ca/anglais/index.htm

Case study 1
Mount Royal College, Calgary

Background
Founded in 1910, Mount Royal College is spread across four city
campuses. With a population of 850,000, Calgary is situated on the

banks of the Bow River and is close to the Rocky Mountains. The 'Calgary Stampede' is probably the city's best-known attraction.

Structure

Mount Royal is one of Alberta's oldest and largest tertiary institutions, serving over 12,000 undergraduates each year. The college offers degrees in business and entrepreneurship, communications, industrial ecology, interior design, non-profit studies and health, and has a world-class conservatory for music and theatre studies.

Social life

Calgary has a range of bars, coffee shops, fast food outlets, cinema, and music venues fitting a city of its size. Its location provides a wide range of outdoor activity options, from snowboarding and skiing in the winter to hiking, biking, horse riding, whitewater rafting and climbing in the summer months.

Applications/accommodation

Mount Royal College has partnership agreements with 35 institutions; where an agreement is in place, you should apply via the appropriate office. Students who aren't attending a partner institution must apply directly to Mount Royal College. Students from outside of Canada can only apply to begin in the Autumn (Fall) semester; while international students already studying in Canada may apply for either of the semesters.

International students lodge in student halls, homestay or private accommodation. On-campus accommodation costs between CAN\$3,600 and CAN\$5,400 a year. Apartment living is also an option, although it's up to the students themselves to find an apartment or house. The Mount Royal College Students' Association keeps an up-to-date list of off-campus housing.

Contact

Prospective Student Services
Office of the Registrar
Mount Royal College
4825 Richard Road SW
Calgary
Alberta T3E 6K6
Canada
Tel: (+1) 403 440 0148
Fax: (+1) 403 440 6740
Email: langinst@mtroyal.ab.ca
Website: http://international.mtroyal.ca

Case study 2
Université de Montréal (UdM) (University of Montreal)

Background
Montreal has a population of 3 million (80 per cent are French speaking) and is renowned for both its rich history and modern, lively cultural activity. Founded in 1878, UdM is ranked second in Canada and is among the top 20 North American universities with over 52,000 students, including 4,000 from 120 foreign countries. UdM ranks second among the 20 Canadian universities for its number of foreign students. Located in a vast park in the heart of Montreal, UdM has been an active part of the city's multicultural urban landscape for the past 125 years.

Structure
There are 13 faculties covering humanities, social sciences, education, the arts, veterinary and natural sciences, offering 270 undergraduate programmes, and exchange programmes with more than 200 international partners.

Social life
Living in Montreal gives you the chance to experience city lifestyle – similar in some respects to being in a large university town in the UK: great nightlife, friendly people (many prefer to speak French), and opportunities for travel and adventure abound. The main feature of Montreal is its bilingual diversity and the distinctive French ambience of the old town. There are numerous restaurants and cafes, museums, galleries and good shopping facilities.

Applications/accommodation
All the necessary information is provided to students with their acceptance letters. For European students, it usually takes from 4–8 weeks to complete all the procedures mentioned above under Application system/visas.

For accommodation, the options are: student residence on campus, renting a room, or taking an apartment (usually unfurnished). There's a student housing complex with rooms for students; these are allocated on a first-come, first-served basis. The residences are single and double room studios. Some have been adapted for people with reduced mobility. Monthly rents are from CAN$206–246 for single rooms and from CAN$361–432 for double occupancy rooms.

Contact
International Liaison
Bernard Landriault
Université de Montréal
Section de Collaborations Internationales
University de Montreal
Quebec
Canada
Tel: (+1) 514 343 7337
Fax: (+1) 514 343 7138
Email: bernard.landriault@umontreal.ca
Website: www.umontreal.ca

Country profile: Czech Republic

Population
10.3 million. The capital, Prague, has a population of 1.21 million.

History/government
Founded in 1993, following the collapse of the former Czechoslovakia. In January 1996 the Czech Republic applied for EU membership, a process which is ongoing and likely to result in full membership in the near future.

Culture, language and lifestyle
Prague is the cultural capital, with a long tradition of music, literature and the arts. The majority of the population is Czech. The language is Czech, although English is used by some universities for certain courses and exchanges. Prague is a cosmopolitan city, with numerous bars and restaurants – the smaller towns and cities reflect tradition, with excellent inexpensive beer and simple dishes of meat and vegetables.

Banking system/currency
The Czech koruna (kop), although from May 2004 the Czech Republic will be part of the EU and the euro (€) will eventually be the national currency. Banking hours are from Monday–Friday, 8am–5pm. ATMs are widely available, especially in Prague.

Climate/geography
The climate is temperate, having mild summers and moderate winters, with snow but little rain. The country is bordered by mountain ranges and is rich in forests, lakes and rivers.

Transport
Prague is at the centre of the country's transport network – the modern international airport has regular flights to most main European/international destinations. Good, inexpensive (if sometimes slow) rail connections link Prague with other parts of the country.

Health arrangements
Health care is free to Czech citizens and those with a long-term resident's permit. Others will usually receive free emergency medical treatment, paying towards the cost of prescribed drugs and dental treatment. If you're planning to spend more than 90 days in the Czech Republic you should contact the National Insurance Contributions Agency to get advice about which benefits are available and transferable. The most important factor is that you must make arrangements for medical matters before you go to the Czech Republic.

Higher education

There are 24 public and 4 state (police and military) higher educational establishments with a total of 187,000 students (3.5 per cent foreign national). There are also 27 private higher education institutions. The Higher Education Act 1990 reinstated academic freedom and introduced shorter degree programmes (bachelor studies). A Bachelor's degree takes 3–4 years.

History of accepting foreign students

Universities are entitled to join the Erasmus/Socrates programme – in recent years, exchanges between UK and Czech Universities have expanded.

Fees

Fees are waived for students participating in an Erasmus/Socrates exchange. Full-time students (UK and European nationals) must pay foreign students' fees, unless they have a scholarship. Fees vary between institutions, ranging from £3,100 to £6,500 per year. If you enrol for a pre-study, one-year Czech course, it will cost around £2,500. Information about study scholarships is available from the Embassy of the Czech Republic.

Working while studying

It's sometimes possible to find part-time work in Prague around the busy tourist industry. Elsewhere it's more difficult, as unemployment is high and you usually need competent knowledge of Czech.

Application system/visas

If you apply as an exchange student, this will be through an institutional/bilateral agreement with your UK university. To apply as a full-time student, contact universities directly, enclosing your CV, a copy of your passport, birth certificate and NHS medical card. Your application should be submitted in February or March.

For stays of up to 180 days, British citizens don't need a visa for the Czech Republic. If you want to stay longer than 180 days, you need to apply for a long-term visa from the Consular Section of the Czech Embassy – these can be issued for one year and are renewable. Applications need to state the purpose of stay, proof of financial resources and accommodation, together with a health certificate.

Expenses/costs

The cost of living, including accommodation (but excluding any fees) is estimated to be £335 monthly, higher in Prague.

Accommodation/assistance

International students are entitled to live in halls and eat in student cafeterias – alternatively, they can rent private accommodation, although this is more expensive and can be difficult to find.

Academic year
This runs in two semesters, September–January and February–June.

Support network
The international office is the main point of contact at universities for international/exchange students. In addition, there are various clubs operating within the National Union of Foreign Students' organisations.

Volume/type of work
You'll need to devote a considerable amount of time to learning the Czech language. As an exchange student you can expect to attend lectures and tutorials, with a lot of time for independent study.

Useful addresses/websites
Council of Higher Education Institutions
Jose Martiho 31
162 52 Prague 6 – Veleslavin
Czech Republic
Tel/Fax: (+420) 220 560 221
Email: arvs@ftvs.cuni.cz
Website: www.radaw.cz

Embassy of the Czech Republic
26 Kensington Palace Gardens
London W6 4QY
Tel· 020 7243 1115
Fax: 020 7243 7926
Email: london@embassy.mzw.cz
Website: www.czechembassy.org.uk/

Institute for Information in Education
Senovazne Namesti 26
PO Box c.1
11006 Czech Republic
Tel: (+ 420) 224 398257
Fax: (+ 420) 224 233 071
Email: info@uni.cz
Website: www.uiv.cz/

Case study
Univerzita Palackého, Olomouc

Background
Olomouc is in the east of the Czech Republic, around four hours by train from Prague. Its historic centre is medieval, with many churches and cultural institutions. The university was founded in 1573, although its modern era dates from 1946.

Structure
The University has seven faculties, and around 15,000 students. It joined Erasmus in 1997, and currently has over 40 bilateral agreements with partners across Europe. There are Czech language courses available, and many in English.

Social life
Olomouc is small and easy to get around. There are many bars and cafes off the central square area – this is the hub of the student social scene. It's within easy reach of Krakow, Vienna and Prague.

Applications/accommodation
Exchange students should apply initially through their home institution. More information on all these matters can be obtained from the university's International Liaison Office.

International or exchange students can stay in one of seven halls. Housing is guaranteed for students from abroad. The halls themselves vary, although normally three students share a room, with two rooms sharing a bathroom. Erasmus students usually live in the same hall.

Contact
International Liaison Office
Univerzita Palackého
Krizkovskeho 77
77147 Olomouc
Czech Republic
Tel: (+420) 585 631062
Fax: (+420) 585 223494
Email: vyhanko@risc.upol.cz
Website: http://www.upol.cz/UP_En/

Country profile: Denmark

Population
5.4 million. Its capital, Copenhagen, has a population of 1.35 million.

History/government
Demark became a Member State of the EEC (now EU) in 1975. It's a constitutional monarchy.

Culture, language and lifestyle
Denmark has four languages: Danish, German, Faroese and Green-landic. Of the population, 85 per cent are urban-based and 15 per cent live rurally. The Danes enjoy culture and there are plenty of museums, arts and music. Traditional Danish food is based on meat and fish served with potatoes and other vegetables, and open sandwiches.

Some 95 per cent of Danes are Catholic. Denmark doesn't have the taboos on alcohol that exist in other Scandinavian countries – the local drink, Akvavit, is consumed in vast quantities. Copenhagen has a vibrant nightlife, but it can be quite quiet elsewhere as social life often focuses on private homes. Since 1989, Denmark has allowed registered partnerships between gay couples.

Banking system/currency
The Danish krone (DKK). Banks are open 10am–4pm Mon–Fri (open until 6pm on Thursdays).

Climate/geography
The country stretches across the Jutland peninsula, with four main islands and more than 400 smaller ones. The climate is generally temperate, with milder winters than its Scandinavian neighbours. Summers can seem cool.

Transport
Denmark has a swift and easy public transport system – trains, buses and ferries are punctual, efficient and well integrated. Cycling is a good option given the flat landscape. In Copenhagen, the city bike scheme allows you to borrow bikes from racks in the city for a deposit of DKK20. The bridge across the Oresund Sound now links Denmark with Sweden.

Health arrangements
You have to pay on the spot for dentists, consultations and prescriptions but can claim the amount back via the E111 (plus passport to the local health centre). You are advised to take out insurance.

Higher education

This is provided by the state, with five general universities and nine specialist institutions; bachelor degrees take three years. Most courses are taught in Danish, but increasingly undergraduate courses are being taught in English.

History of accepting foreign students

Danish society is a very welcoming one, but learning the language can be an issue. With more courses coming on stream in English (including chemistry, law, history and economics), this situation may change.

Fees

In general there are no tuition fees payable for higher education courses.

Working while studying

This should be possible under EU employment rules.

Application system/visas

You should apply direct to the institution by 15 March for entry in September, or apply in September for January entry. All foreign students must satisfy the intended institution of competence in Danish by taking the Danskproeve II exam before being accepted.

EU students staying for more that three months need to apply to the Danish Embassy in their home country for a residence permit. Danish immigration authorities require you to provide financial details from your bank, showing that you have the equivalent of DKK4,200 monthly available to support yourself. Once you have a permanent address you need to register with the local civil authorities. The university international office can help you with all of this. (There are different arrangements for nationals of other Nordic countries.)

Expenses/costs

The University of Copenhagen suggests the following monthly guidance: housing: DKK1,800–2,800; food and bills: DKK1,500–2,000; books: DKK210; transport: DKK350; and pocket money: DKK1,000.

Accommodation/assistance

Accommodation is high quality, and all the higher education institutions have halls costing around €250 a month. You should apply direct to the institution for more details.

Academic year

There are two semesters, running from September–January, and February–June.

Support network
There is an active and wide range of student unions. Universities also run mentoring schemes to help you ease into studying there.

Volume/type of work
Seen as quite heavy – there are lectures (often quite large-scale) and assessment is frequently exam-based (both written and oral). Some courses also have assessed written work and oral assignments during the semester. Assessment in Denmark is by way of a graded 13-point scale, and if you're on an exchange, you need to be clear how your home institution will require your work to be assessed – it's best to discuss this with your department or international office.

Useful addresses/websites
Ministry of Education
Fredricksholm Kanal 21
1220 Copenhagen K
Denmark
Tel: (+45) 33 92 52 20
Fax: (+45) 33 92 55 47
Email: uvm@uvm.dk
Website: www.uvm.dk

Royal Danish Embassy
55 Sloane Street
London SW1X 9SR
Tel: 020 7333 0200
Fax: 020 7333 0270
Email: lonamb@um.dk
Website: www.denmark.org.uk

Case study
Københavns Universitet
(University of Copenhagen)

Background
Founded 1479 and the oldest university in Denmark, it enrolled its first female student in 1877. It now has 33,000 students and is located at a number of sites, mainly in Copenhagen. The city is lively, has an excellent music scene and is compact and easy to get to know.

Structure
Six main faculties with 7,700 academic and support staff. It offers

a wide range of courses in English each year (check the university website: www.ku.dk, as plans are made on a semester-by-semester basis). The international office is geared towards helping exchange students and can guide you on courses in English and other details.

Social life
Excellent in and around Copenhagen, but Denmark can seem rather quieter outside the capital.

Applications/accommodation
For exchanges, contact the international office at your home institution. For full-time study you should read the guide *Rules for Admission of Foreign Students*, which is available from the Foreign Students' Office. The international office is also very helpful on practical and academic issues for both full-time and exchange students, and organises orientation weeks four times a year.

Contact
Foreign Students' Office
Studieadministrationen
Københavns Universitet
Fiolstraede 22
DK-1171 København K
Denmark
Tel: (+45) 35 32 28 92
Fax: (+45) 35 32 39 00
Email: inter@adm.ku.dk
Website: www.ku.dk/english/

Country profile: Finland

Population
15.5 million. The capital, Helsinki, has a population of 500,000.

History/government
Finland become independent after the Russian Revolution of 1917, but was attacked by the Soviet Union in 1939. The neutral stance it was forced to adopt lasted until the disintegration of the Soviet Union in 1991. Finland is a republic with a single chamber of parliament.

Culture, language and lifestyle
Finnish and Swedish are both its official languages. Lapp is spoken in the far north. Finland has a great commitment to culture, particularly music and the arts. The Finns place a high value on fresh food: fish is very popular, particularly smoked fish, and you'll also find reindeer or elk on the menu. Alcohol is very expensive and highly regulated.

Finns enjoy a very high standard of living. Sport is very popular and, of course, the sauna originated in Finland, providing a place to relax and meet friends.

Banking system/currency
The euro (€). All financial transactions take place through banks so you'll have to open an account. The service account and savings accounts are most practical for students. Most banks have self-service payment machines through which you can pay bills, as generally, Finns do not use cheques. Banks are generally open Mon–Fri, 9.15am–4.15pm. There are plenty of ATMs available.

Climate/geography
It is a low-lying country, two-thirds of which is covered by forest. The coastline is deeply indented and there are many small islands and over 60,000 lakes. The climate is very severe during the winter but summer days are very long, dry and hot.

Transport
The main airport is Helsinki-Vantaa; internal flights are important because of the harsh climate. Long-distance buses run frequently, although most of the roads are in the south. Finland has a very good rail network. Students can obtain discounts on most forms of transport with a Student Union card.

Health arrangements
Finland has top-quality health care. Student health needs are looked after by the Finnish student health service, the YHTS. Student Union

(HYY) membership gives you entitlement to free or low cost medical and dental care, but this doesn't cover hospital treatment (for which charges are made on the same basis as for Finnish nationals). You should take out private health insurance before travel.

Higher education

Over 60 per cent of students go on to higher education in universities and polytechnics. A Bachelor's degree is awarded for 120 credits – students are expected to gain between 15 and 20 credits each semester. The minimum period of study is three years, but on average students take around six years.

History of accepting foreign students

Finnish universities have welcomed foreign students for some time through bilateral agreements and exchanges, but the language barrier can be an issue. Some courses are now aimed at international students, with a growing number taught in English. Nevertheless, you'll need some proficiency in Finnish if you're to get the most out of your stay.

Fees

There are no admission or course fees, but students might be charged for tuition materials.

Working while studying

A work permit is included in the residence permit for EU students, with no restrictions on the number of hours that can be worked.

Application system/visas

As an independent student you should apply to the institution of your choice at least a year beforehand, as the system isn't centralised. Along with your grades, you might also have to take an entrance examination. No study permit or visa is required for EU students for periods of up to three months. You must apply within three days of arrival for a 'Notice of Moving'; you can get this from any post office. For stays of over three months, a residence permit is needed: apply to the Finnish Embassy before you travel, providing proof of your ability to support yourself and other documents.

Expenses/costs

Life is expensive in Finland. Total monthly living costs for a single Finnish student, allowing for food, transport and accommodation, are around €673. Student Union membership is compulsory, costing between €45 and €85 annually, but this is free for exchange students. Allow for insurance costs: this can be arranged through ISIS. Also, don't forget that you'll need to buy warmer clothing.

Accommodation/assistance
Rented accommodation is in short supply and expensive; many students live at home. The usual form of accommodation is the student housing foundation – a room in a shared apartment costing €220–225 monthly, including utilities. Accommodation for exchange students is usually arranged by the host institution. Independent students will receive an application form when offered a place; to be sure of getting accommodation, you should apply by the end of June.

Academic year
There are two semesters, running from September–December, and January–May.

Support network
There is no uniform support network. On arrival you'll be offered an orientation programme, and while you're studying, support could be provided by a student tutor from the Students' Union, or perhaps a foreign students' adviser.

Volume/type of work
Programmes of study don't follow a standard pattern, so it's hard to generalise about the work that's required. Degree programmes provide guidelines but students can follow them at their own pace, and even replace lecture courses with independent study. Finnish universities are traditionally hierarchical, with lectures being the chief means of instruction, but they're adopting a more participatory style of learning. In this environment, students need to take control of their learning and to use their own initiative.

Useful addresses/websites
Centre for International Mobility (CIMO)
Hakaniemenkatu 2
PO Box 343
00531 Helsinki
Finland
Tel: (+358) 9 7747 7033
Fax: (+358) 9 7747 7064
Email: socrates@cimo.fi
Website: www.cimo.fi

Finnish Embassy
38 Chesham Place
London SW1X 8HW
Tel: 020 7838 6200
Fax: 020 7235 3680
Email: Sanomat.Ion@formin.fi

Website: www.finemb.org.uk

Finnish Institute
35–36 Eagle Street
London WC1R 4AJ
Tel: 020 7404 3309
Fax: 020 7404 8893
Email: info@finnish-institute.org.uk
Website: www.finnish-institute.org.uk

Case study
Helsingin Yliopisto (University of Helsinki)

Background
Founded in 1640, the university is the oldest and largest in Finland and an important centre of research. It moved to Helsinki in 1825.

Structure
There are nine faculties with over 34,000 students, with 1,192 foreign students and 734 exchange students. The language of instruction is mainly Finnish or Swedish, but faculties do offer some courses in English. For details, see the homepage of the faculty or the ECTS guidebooks.

Social life
There is an active student social life with the usual range of clubs and societies. Seasonal parties are a feature of student life, such as the 'ultimate drinking fest'. The city is lively, with bars, restaurants and free music in the parks.

Applications/accommodation
Independent students should apply using the form downloaded from the *International Applicants' Guide* (www.helsinki.fi/english/intrel.information.htm). Check requirements and deadlines with specific faculties. It's possible that you will have to pass a very selective entrance examination in addition to your grades. The International Student Services department will give general advice.

If you're an independent student, you can apply to the Student Housing Foundation (see the university's website for more information). As a potential exchange student, you should approach your own institution (accommodation is provided for exchange students in halls).

Contact
Student Exchange Manager
International Student Services
University of Helsinki
PO Box 33 (YliopistonKatu 4)
00014 Finland
Tel: (+358) 9 191 22177
Fax: (+358) 9 191 22662
Email: robert.ramberg@helsinki.fi (Foreign Student Adviser)
Website: www.helsinki.fi/english

Country profile: France

Population
Population over 59 million. The capital, Paris, has a population of 2.2 million.

History/government
Modern France began in 1789 with the French Revolution and the declaration of a republic in 1792. After war throughout Europe, Napoleon was declared Emperor in 1803. The history of 19th-century France was turbulent. The country was devastated in the First World War, despite being one of the victors. Defeat in the Second World War led to occupation by Germany. Since 1945 the history of France has been more stable. France was a founder member of the EEC in 1957.

Culture, language and lifestyle
Traditionally, France has been famous for good food and wine, with a growing appreciation of regional produce. The French are immensely proud of their national culture, and have a strong sense of national identity. The French have fought hard against being overwhelmed by other countries' media, especially film. France has become a leader in technological advance in Europe, for example, in aerospace, transport and telecommunications.

France is still a centralised country with an appreciation of bureaucracy, despite the growing importance of its regions. Fashion and style are highly important, as are food and wine. Sports such as cycling, football and rugby are very popular.

Banking system/currency
The euro (€). The banking system is similar to that of the UK. The two accounts most suitable for students are current and savings accounts. To open an account, a foreigner must be staying for over three months. For under three months, a savings bank or the Post Office can be used.

Banks are generally open 9am–4.30pm. In small towns they may close for lunch.

Climate/geography
The country is crossed by great rivers including the Seine, Loire and Rhône. The Channel coast has a typically north-west European climate, while the Mediterranean experiences scorching summers and warm, wet winters.

Transport
The French transport network is highly advanced. Paris–Charles de Gaulle is the main airport. Other minor airports have expanded with

the growth of low-cost airlines. The railway system is excellent. SNCF trains form the main network, and fast TGV trains connect major cities. Eurostar links Paris with the UK and Belgium. Motorways connect all areas, although tolls are payable.

Health arrangements

Costs are covered through the social security system. You should take a form E111 with you to cover emergency treatment. If you are under 28 and studying at a recognised university, you'll be eligible for the Student Health Plan, which provides cover for up to 70 per cent of all medical costs. You'll also be offered insurance to cover the difference between what is charged and the actual cost.

Higher education

There are two routes in higher education: vocational courses last for two years, and academic study is organised in cycles. The first cycle is a two-year general studies programme preparing students for the DEUG (the Diplôme d'études universitaires générales – the foundation level qualification in the French university system). The second and third cycles each take one year, and are offered by universities or *Grandes Ecoles*. At the end of the third year, students are awarded the *Licence* and after the fourth year the *Maîtrise*.

History of accepting foreign students

French universities have always accepted foreign students, but there will be few allowances for English speakers.

Fees

EU students pay no tuition fees at French state universities, but do have to pay an annual administration fee.

Working while studying

Students from EU countries don't need a work permit. Any foreign student wishing to work in France must be enrolled at an institution that's approved for entitlement under the standard students' health insurance scheme. Often, offers of work will be posted at the CNOUS–CROUS site (see below).

Application system/visas

For exchange programmes, contact your home institution's international office. If you want to apply independently for a place on the first cycle, you must follow a special preliminary assessment procedure. Information and application forms are available from L'Institut Français in London. For the second and third cycles, you should contact institutions directly. Qualifications that are acceptable in the UK are generally fine for a similar course in France, but there can be specific requirements, such as an entrance examination. Most courses are taught and assessed in French: full-time students must pass a language proficiency test.

A study permit or visa is not needed, but you will require a temporary residence permit for stays lasting over three months. These permits can be obtained from the local town hall or police station.

Expenses/costs
These depend on the region and lifestyle. In 2003, costs were estimated to be anywhere between €250 and €500 monthly.

Accommodation/assistance
All full-time foreign students are entitled to a room in a hall of residence managed by CROUS. This will cost between €155 and €300 monthly. An application form will be sent when an offer of a place has been made. Exchange students will probably have to look on the open market. A private source of accommodation is the Foyers d'Étudiants.

Academic year
This is in two semesters: October–January and February–June.

Support network
As well as their other functions, CROUS perform a more general support and advisory role. The same type of support isn't available in France as it is in the UK. There's no Student Union, but there is the usual range of clubs and societies. Much of student life takes place in bars, clubs and cafes. A useful source of information for foreign students is the Service Universitaires pour Étudiants Étrangers.

Volume/type of work
Programmes of work can be quite intense – depending on the type of university you go to, generally, academic work is more theoretically based than in the UK.

Useful addresses/websites
Centre National des Oeuvres Universitaires et Scolaires (CNOUS)/ Centre Regionale des Oeuvres Universitaires et Scolaires (CROUS)
69 Quai d'Orsay
75340 Paris Cedex 7
France
Tel: (+33) 1 44 18 53 00
Fax: (+33) 1 44 18 53 63
Email: direction@cnous.fr, com@cnous.fr
Website: www.cnous.fr

Égide
28 rue de la Grange-Aux-Belles

75010 Paris
France
Tel: (+33) 1 40 40 58 58
Fax: (+33) 1 42 41 85 90
Email: contact@egide.asso.fr
Website: www.egide.asso.fr/

French Embassy
58 Knightsbridge
London SW1X 7JT
Tel: 020 7201 1000
Fax: 020 7073 1355
Email: presse.londres-amba@diplomatie.fr
Website: www.ambafrance-uk.org

L'Institut Français
14 Cromwell Place
South Kensington
London SW7 2JR
Tel: 020 7581 2701
Email: box.office@ambafrance.org.uk
Website: www.institut.ambafrance.org.uk

Case study 1
Université d'Avignon et des Pays de Vaucluse

Background

Avignon is a beautiful city enclosed by 4km of medieval walls, situated beside the River Rhône. Founded in 1303, the university still uses many of the old buildings although it moved to a new site, Saint-Marthe, in 1997.

Structure

The largest faculty within the university is Lettres et Sciences Humaines. The three other faculties are Sciences Exactes et Sciences de la Nature, Sciences et Langages Appliqués, and Sciences Juridiques, Politiques et Economiques. There are also two institutes. In 2002–3 there were 7,175 students so it doesn't feel impersonal and overcrowded. The new buildings are buzzing, but spacious.

French is the language used for teaching and assessment and no special provisions are made for English speakers. For exchange students, French courses at an appropriate level are provided at the beginning of each semester, while for other students, a course runs throughout the year.

Social life

Social life mainly takes place in the bars and cafes of the old city. The university also provides a range of sporting activities to students with a student card and proof of fitness.

Applications/accommodation

For admission exchanges, contact your own university's international office. If you're an independent student, there are different procedures to be followed, depending on whether you wish to be admitted to a course in the first or second cycle – more information can be provided by the Services des Relations Internationales.

Student accommodation is organised by the CROUS. There are three residences near the Saint-Marthe campus, and CROUS can also supply a list of private sector accommodation. Apply before mid-June for the first semester, and mid-December for the second semester.

Contact

Services des Relations Internationales
Université d'Avignon et des Pays de Vaucluse
74 rue Louis Pasteur
Case 10
Avignon Cedex 1
France
Tel: (+33) 4 90 16 25 58
Fax: (+33) 4 90 16 25 60
Email: sri@univ-avignon.fr
Website: http://www.univ-avignon.fr/

Case study 2
Université de Nice Sophia Antipolis

Background

UNSA became an independent institution in 1965. It's now a dynamic centre working in partnership with businesses and research establishments. Nice is the capital of the Riviera, although it still has an old town and port.

Structure

As well as nine faculties providing research and teaching at UNSA, there are three separate schools. In 2002 there were about 26,500 students, including 2,400 foreign students. Teaching is generally in French, apart from a few specialised courses. The EFE service (French for Foreigners) provides courses at the beginning of each semester for exchange students, and also regularly during the year. A placement test determines level of instruction.

Social life

Many sporting activities are available for a very reasonable price, cheap tickets for the theatre, opera and cinema and many free activities (the Espace Étudiants link on the UNSA website gives details).

Applications/accommodation

Exchange programmes are handled by the International Relations Department, who will contact you once information has been received from your university. To make a direct application for a place on the first cycle of a degree programme, write to the Service Scolarité des Étudiants Étrangers.

Accommodation in Nice is generally expensive. A room in halls will cost between €124 and €138 monthly, and in private accommodation, €350 and €550. CROUS will send you an accommodation form once your application has been accepted.

Contact

Direction des Relations Internationales
Université de Nice Sophia Antipolis
28 Avenue Valrose
Boîte Postale 2135
01603 Nice Cedex 2
France
Tel: (+33) 4 92 07 60 60
Fax: (+33) 4 92 07 66 00
Email: etudiants-RI@unice.fr
Website: www.unice.fr

Country profile: Germany

Population
82 million. The capital, Berlin, has a population of 3.5 million.

History/government
East and West German unification took place in October 1990.

Culture, language and lifestyle
Culturally, a traditional country with a strong belief in the importance of order and thoroughness. Regional identity is very important. There is no national daily newspaper and television is organised on a regional basis. Food is substantial, and Germans take their cuisine seriously. Standard German is spoken throughout the country and it's important to get to know the language as a means of social integration.

German people are serious and hard-working, but enjoy broad humour and opportunities for fun. Drunken behaviour is not generally appreciated.

Banking system/currency
The euro (€). A current account (*Girokonto*) is the most appropriate for students. The EC-Card enables cash to be taken out at ATMs. Banks are open 9am–4pm weekdays, although some close for lunch.

Climate/geography
This is varied: the North is characterised by lakes and moorland, while the South has hills and large lakes and the German section of the Alps. The main rivers are the Rhine, Elbe and Danube. Germany has a continental climate.

Transport
There has been a rapid growth in air transport. High-speed rail services are an attractive means of travel between cities; metropolitan railway networks have also been extended and linked with bus, tram and underground systems in most urban areas.

Health arrangements
The health care system ensures virtually universal access to a wide range of services. Cover is provided by statutory or private health insurance schemes. Students have to present proof of health insurance before registration at the university. Any doctors' visits, stays in hospital and treatment are free of charge.

Higher education
Study at the *Gymnasium* leads on to university. A certificate from the

Realschüle leads to the *Fachschüle*, then the *Fachhochschüle* (technical university). This is preferred because of the length of study and more practical nature of the courses. Few university courses have a fixed curriculum or duration, and students choose their order and length of study. Universities generally award the academic degrees of *Diplom* and *Magister* as well as the doctorate.

History of accepting foreign students
The number of foreign students at German universities is high.

Fees
Usually, students from the EU don't pay any tuition fees.

Working while studying
A student from the EU doesn't need a work permit and there are no limits to the number of hours that can be worked. The local employment exchange will have a student job location department, sometimes on the premises of student services.

Application system/visas
Most UK students study in Germany as part of an exchange. Independent students need to show their competence in German through a language proficiency test. Those planning to spend only one semester are exempt. Application for most subjects must be made to the Foreign Students' Office of the institution concerned. Some courses (Numerus Clausus, NC) have restricted and competitive entry. For these, application must be made to the ZVS (Central Office for the Allocation of Study Places). For EU nationals, a visa isn't required, but if you plan to stay for more than three months (and to get a residence permit) you must register your permanent address within one week of arrival at the Resident Registration Bureau – the Einwohnermeldeamt.

Expenses/costs
Germany is a fairly expensive place to study. You'll need to allow €660 monthly for basic expenses. The semester fee must also be paid to obtain the Seminar Card. This costs around €100 and goes towards financing the student services association, as well as the Students' Union.

Accommodation/assistance
The best accommodation is provided by student halls run by *Studentwerk* organisations. These are non-profit making, so rents are favourable. Monthly rent (including utilities) costs between €150 and €300, depending on quality and location.

Academic year
This runs in two semesters from October–March and April–September.

Support network

The *Studentwerk* organisations take care of the economic, social, health care and cultural support of students in most higher education institutions. Look out for the special service packages for foreign students to make life easier – costing between €150 and €320 monthly.

Volume/type of work

The amount of work demanded annually by a traditional university course depends in part on the student's commitment. Students who wish to undertake paid employment can opt for a lighter workload and take fewer units each year. This would prolong the period of their studies. German students are usually older than in the UK and greater independence is expected. Universities have a greater research focus; courses require students to work on their own more, with long examinations. A course at a *Fachhochschüle* will be shorter and more practical, with a specified curriculum.

Useful addresses/websites

German Academic Exchange Service
34 Belgrave Square
London SW1X 8QB
Tel: 020 7235 1736
Fax: 020 7235 9602
Email: info@daad.org.uk
Websites: www.london.daad.de
www.campus-germany.de

German Embassy
23 Belgrave Square
London SW1X 8PZ
Tel: 020 7824 1300
Fax: 020 7824 1435
Email: mail@german-embassy.org.uk
Website: www.german-embassy.org.uk

Goethe Institute
50 Princes Gate
Exhibition Road
London SW7 2PH
Tel: 020 7596 4000
Email: mail@london.goethe.de/london
Website: www.goethe.de/lon/enindex.htm
www.zvs.de
www.higher-education-compass.de
www.studentenwerke.de
www.student-affairs.de

Case study 1
Freie Universität Berlin

Background

Founded after the Second World War, the university is the largest in Berlin and one of the largest in the country.

Structure

FU Berlin has 12 departments covering the main academic subjects and three central interdisciplinary institutes. With 43,500 students and around 90 different courses of study, it attracts students from Germany and beyond. The ratio of teaching staff to students is high. More than 10 per cent of all FU Berlin students come from abroad. German is the teaching language, but there is language training at all levels and some courses are taught in English. A special feature of FU Berlin is the student-run and designed Project Tutorial Programme to support course-work, as independent learning is important.

Social life

Berlin has been growing fast since becoming the nation's capital again and there is no shortage of interesting and exciting activities. On campus there are student organisations, orchestras and choirs as well as theatre groups. There is also uniRadio. The Centre for Recreational Sports is popular, offering around 600 different activities.

Applications/accommodation

Most students from the UK take courses at FU Berlin as part of an exchange programme. Applications and accommodation are mostly handled for them by the student's home university and the institution they are applying to. Independent students have different methods of application, whether you wish to study on a course with limited numbers (NC) or with open admission. For the former, apply directly to the Freie Universität. For NC courses, EU students must apply to the ZVS.

Accommodation is organised by *Studentwerk* Berlin. Single rooms with shared kitchens, bathrooms, and laundry cost from €125 monthly. Apply as soon as you've been offered a place. Rooms in the private market cost from €200–250 monthly, including utilities.

Contact
Admissions Office
Freie Universität Berlin
Zulassungsbüro 1
Iltisstrasse1
D-14195 Berlin
Germany
Tel : (+49) 30 838 75521
Email: erasmus@zedat.fu-berlin.de
Website: www.fu-berlin.de or www.student-affairs.de

Case study 2
Ruprecht-Karls-Universität Heidelberg
(University of Heidelberg)

Background
Founded in 1386, the university is the oldest in Germany (and one of the oldest in Europe), as well as one of the most important research centres in the country. The city is located beautifully on the River Neckar at the foot of the Odenwald, with a Renaissance-period castle at its centre. The university buildings are distributed around the city, with many to be found in the old town.

Structure
Fifteen faculties embracing the arts and sciences, including law and medicine. Degrees awarded include the *Magister* and *Diplom*; courses are mainly taught in German, although more courses are now in English. International students make up around 20 per cent of the 24,000 students that are enrolled.

Social life
Much of student life takes place in the taverns and cafes of the old town. *Studentenwerk* caters for many areas of student life, including the Heidelberg Network programme, excursions and social events. Other student organisations also provide a range of activities including sport.

Applications/accommodation
Most students from the UK will be studying in Heidelberg as part of an exchange; their institutions will help. Independent students apply to the Akademisches Auslandsamt using a form which they can download from the Internet. Application deadlines are mid-July for the winter semester, and mid-January for summer.

Studentenwerk Heidelberg has put together a package of services to help students: the two modules (which must be booked in advance) include a choice of single rooms in halls, a Campuscard and semester ticket. Students staying for one or two semesters will be considered only if the packages are not booked up by students staying for longer, but they'll still be helped with accommodation and be eligible for support services.

Contact

Akademisches Auslandsamt
Ruprecht-Karls-Universität Heidelberg
Seminarstrasse 2
69117 Heidelberg
Germany
Tel: (+49) 62 21 54-0
Fax: (+49) 62 21 54-2618
Email: gb@zuv.uni-heidelberg. de
Website: www.zuv.uni-heidelberg.de

Country profile: Greece

Population
10.6 million. The capital, Athens, has a population of 3.1 million.

History/government
After heavy resistance to German occupation during the Second World War, civil war took place from 1946–9. A military regime was established in 1967, finally falling in 1974 after much unrest. Greece then rejected the monarchy and became a parliamentary republic.

Culture, language and lifestyle
Greek civilisation emerged around 1300BC. Its art, architecture, philosophy, literature and music have greatly influenced Western culture, and the Greek Orthodox Church plays a central role. Greek food is based on simple, fresh ingredients that are freshly prepared. Lamb and poultry are the most popular meats, plus a wide range of fish and fresh vegetables. The majority speak modern Greek.

The Greeks are family-oriented. The lifestyle is relaxed, being influenced by the warm Mediterranean climate, and based primarily outdoors. Village life remains simple, but towns and cities are lively and congested.

Banking system/currency
The euro (€). Banks are usually open in the mornings, and ATMs widely available.

Climate/geography
Greece has around 13,676 km of coastline with sea on three sides. It's predominantly rural and much of the land consists of mountain ranges. The numerous islands are stony and dry. The climate has hot dry summers and mild wet winters, apart from the damper mountain regions of the west. There's snow in the winter in the higher mountains.

Transport
There are major airports at Athens, Thessaloniki and Rhodes. Rail travel is quite good between major centres, but in other areas it's slow. A major programme of road construction is under way. The bus network operates throughout the country (be sure to book for long journeys). Ferries, hydrofoils and catamarans will take you to the islands – slower is cheaper.

Health arrangements
Medical care is free for all registered students, who are given a personal health care card entitling them to free consultations with a doctor, as

well as some free medication and hospital treatment. Take an E111 with you, and be sure to get medical insurance before going too.

Higher education
Higher education is divided into universities (Anotata Ekpaideutiks Idriamata, AEI) and technological education institutes (TEI). Admission is judged according to performance in national examinations; study for an undergraduate degree usually takes between 4 and 6 years, and at a TEI, a minimum of three years.

History of accepting foreign students
International students usually arrive as part of exchange programmes with some special arrangements to assist study, such as being allowed to write essays in English. Teaching is usually in Greek, except for a few programmes for international students.

Fees
There are no tuition fees for British students.

Working while studying
There's no barrier to students working while studying. Seasonal workers are always needed by the tourist industry, but don't rely on funding your studies this way.

Application system/visas
The university admission system is centralised; the number of students to be admitted is specified by the government. To study full degrees at Greek universities you must apply to the Ministry of Education and Religious Affairs. You don't need to pass the national entrance examination, but there is a special examination which is set every September. There might be other restrictions imposed by faculties, and you need to show competence in the Greek language. Exchange students should approach their home universities. EU students don't need a study permit or visa, but to stay longer than three months, you'll need to get a residence permit from the Greek Embassy or from the Aliens' Department after arrival.

Expenses/costs
The cost of living is fairly low in Greece: accommodation and subsistence should cost no more than €290–435 monthly. Subsidised catering also reduces living costs: all students are entitled to two free meals a day at university cafeterias.

Accommodation/assistance
Greek universities have some halls, with 8 per cent of places reserved for foreign students. Apply to the institution after an offer of a place has been made.

Academic year
This is run in two semesters, October–January and February–June.

Support network
Most universities have student support services as well as facilities for foreign students.

Volume/type of work
This is heavy, with emphasis on examinations for assessment. Much of the work is theoretical in nature and traditionally academic.

Useful addresses/websites
Greek Embassy
1a Holland Park
London W11 3TP
Tel: 020 7221 6467
Fax: 020 7243 3202
Email: consulategeneral@greekembassy.org.uk
Website: www.greekembassy.org.uk

Ministry of Education and Religious Affairs
Mitropoleos 15
10185 Athens
Greece
Tel: (+30) 1 0323 7480
Fax: (+30) 1 0322 0767
Email: webmaster@ypepth.gr
Website: www.ypepth.gr

Case study
University of Athens

Background
The first university to be founded in the new Greek state. Originally sited near the Acropolis, in the 1960s a new campus was built in Ilissia and further branches are now at Goudi and Daphne.

Structure
The university has five faculties and 80,000 students, making it among the largest in the EU; it also has bilateral exchange agreements with over 260 other European universities. Courses are long – it takes four years to get a diploma (equivalent to a bachelor's degree). Teaching is normally in Greek but other

languages can be used. Special arrangements may be made for exchanges.

Social life

Athens is chaotic, but fascinating. Go to the Pláka for a lively evening, but not if you're short of money! And don't forget that Athens is hosting the 2004 Olympics, which will affect prices and congestion. The university club is the centre of social life; there's also a sports activities centre. The counselling centre handles all matters concerning student life, and there's an Erasmus/ Socrates office for information and advice.

Applications/accommodation

To apply, exchange students should consult their own institution at first. Students who want to enrol for full degree programmes should apply to the Ministry of Education and Religious Affairs (see above).

There isn't enough accommodation in halls, so foreign students normally spend the first few days in budget-priced hostels or hotels. Details are provided after 1 September: lists of people offering apartments or rooms are available then. A shared apartment costs around €180 monthly.

Contact

European and International Relations Department
University of Athens
Main Building
30 Panepistimiou El.Venizelou Street
10679 Athens
Greece
Tel: (+30) 21 0368 9713
Fax: (+30) 21 0368 9720
Email: Socrates@interel.uoa.gr/socrates-erasmus
Website: www.interel.uoa.gr

Country profile: Hungary

Population
10.3 million. The capital, Budapest, has a population of 1.91 million.

History/government
After the Second World War, the communists gained power and the 1956 uprising was violently suppressed. A new constitution was approved in 1989 and the first free parliamentary elections took place in 1990. Hungary is now a parliamentary democracy, with a president as head of state and a prime minister.

Culture, language and lifestyle
Hungarian is spoken by 96 per cent of the population. Meat features heavily on menus, often with onions and sour cream – favourites are goulash and paprika chicken with dumplings. Hungarian culture has an international reputation and there will be nationwide celebrations of its entry into the EU in 2004.

There is a big difference between life in Budapest and the rest of the country. Budapest is a lively European city and the centre of national life; the other cities are much smaller. Lakes and rivers provide popular resorts. Music is important at major festivals or folk performances.

Banking system/currency
The Hungarian forint (Ft), although after Hungary's entrance into the EU the euro (€) will eventually become the national currency. Banks are generally open from Monday–Friday, 8am–4pm, and ATMs are reasonably widespread. The usual credit cards are accepted, although it is unwise to rely on this outside cities.

Climate/geography
The Great Plain dominates the landscape, and the Danube flows from the south through Budapest. Hungary has a continental climate: in summer it's very hot, while in winter it can fall below 0°C. Rainfall and temperature vary considerably, and there can be much snow in winter.

Transport
Most transport networks radiate from Budapest (the main airport is Ferihegy). The train network offers different classes of travel (seats must be reserved for inter-city services). There are few motorways, so major roads can be very busy. For cross-country journeys, buses are probably the best option. Students are given discounts on public transport.

Health arrangements

Emergency treatment is free for UK citizens, but there's a flat rate charge for medicines. First aid and ambulance services are also free in emergencies, with charges for further treatment. Dental and optical services are paid treatments. Private health insurance is essential: international students without an accepted form of insurance must take out insurance in Hungary and pay for a medical check-up.

Higher education

This is currently being transformed to prepare for entry into the EU in 2004. It traditionally took place in smaller institutions, but the numbers have now been reduced and reforms made. Apart from those institutions run by churches and other bodies, the network is made up of state-run organisations. Courses usually last five or six years, leading to a diploma.

History of accepting foreign students

Foreign students do attend Hungarian universities but the language is a barrier although some degree courses are taught in English.

Fees

Vary depending on the institution and course but usually from US$2,000–4,500.

Working while studying

At present students are not allowed to work on a study visa but this will change after Hungary's entry into the EU.

Application system/visas

Hungarian universities can join the Erasmus/Socrates programme, so for exchange study you should approach your own university. Independent applicants must have completed education in your own country to university entrance level; apply direct to the institution in which you are interested. Getting a place is competitive: you must pass an entrance exam and show competence in Hungarian for most courses.

To attend university you must have a student visa from the Hungarian Embassy. This allows a one-year stay; during the first 15 days, students need to get a temporary residence permit.

Expenses/costs

These vary according to location and lifestyle. A rented apartment will cost around US$100–150 monthly and a dormitory room around US$100, including utilities. Other expenses are a deposit for the student ID card and on lodgings.

Accommodation/assistance
Accommodation can be in halls, dormitories or rented apartments. However, there are a limited number of dormitory places available and rooms are often shared. It's best to apply when you've received an offer to study.

Academic year
This is in two semesters, September–December and February–May.

Support network
This is provided by the International Students Centre and the Students' Union (HÖK) which organises social, cultural and sporting life and manages the student institutions. Other sections provide support and counselling.

Volume/type of work
Tends to be heavy, traditional and academic. The style of instruction is formal, but current reforms could change this.

Useful addresses/websites
Hungarian Cultural Centre
10 Maiden Lane
London WC2E 7NA
Tel: 020 7240 8448
Fax: 020 7240 4847
Email: culture@hungary.org.uk
Website: www.hungary.org.uk/start.htm

Hungarian Embassy
35b Eaton Place
London SW1X 8BY
Tel: 020 7235 4448
Fax: 020 7823 1348
Email: hunpress@huemblon.org.uk
Website: www.huemblon.org.uk

Case study
Budapesti Müszaki és Gazdasátudomábyi Egyetem
(Budapest University of Technology and Economics)

Background
Situated centrally in Budapest. The university developed from an institution established in 1782 to train engineers, attaining

university status in 1871. It merged with the Technical University in 1967.

Structure

The university has eight faculties with 15,859 students enrolled in 2000. Most international students belong to the International Education Centre. All the faculties offer degree courses in English and other languages, but Hungarian is used for most degrees.

Social life

A wide variety of activities is available. The Students' International Union (SIU) is a main provider with its own athletic and football club and swimming pool. Budapest has a huge range of activities from folk music, clubs, cinemas, theatres, orchestras and cultural festivals.

Applications/accommodation

For exchanges, approach your own university first. Applications from independent students are accepted partly on the basis of secondary school final reports and partly on the results of the university's placement test, which is taken in the third week of the academic year. Forms can be downloaded from the website. Enrolment takes place in the first week of September.

There are seven student hostels/dormitories; availability is limited. Most Erasmus students are put up in a hostel for a week or so after arrival, and rented accommodation in the city is handled by rental agencies. You can get advice on accommodation from the agency run by university students in the first week of September. The SIU provides information on this, as well as support.

Contact

The Registrar
Budapest University of Technology and Economics
International Education Centre
1521 Budapest
Hungary
Tel: (+36) 1 463 3548
Fax: (+36) 1463 1110
Email: Admissions@tanok.bme.hu
Website: www.tanok.bme.hu

Country profile: Republic of Ireland

Population
3.8 million. The capital, Dublin, has a population of 1 million.

History/government
After a long historical association with Britain, with many periods of conflict, Ireland became a republic in 1948 and joined the EEC (now EU) in 1981.

Culture, language and lifestyle
Ireland has a strong Gaelic heritage and is famous for literature and sports such as hurling and Gaelic football. Its official languages are English and Irish Gaelic, and the influence of the Roman Catholic Church remains strong. St Patrick's Day (17 March) is a focal point for celebration; Ireland is noted for its friendliness. Food is traditionally fresh and wholesome, and Guinness is the main alcoholic drink. The pace of life is slow and relaxed, especially in rural areas.

Banking system/currency
The euro (€). Banking opening hours are similar to those in the UK; there are widespread ATM facilities.

Climate/geography
A picturesque country, with small mountains around the coast and many lakes (loughs) inland. The west coast is especially dramatic, with deep valleys and steep cliffs. Ireland has a typical island climate with mild winters, cool summers and significant rainfall.

Transport
Many airlines, including low cost carriers, provide frequent flights from the UK to Dublin International, the country's major airport. You can also travel by boat to Ireland. There are good rail and bus links between all major centres, although road travel can be slow, especially in rural areas.

Health arrangements
UK nationals are entitled to free emergency medical treatment. However, this doesn't cover routine visits to the GP (around €20 per visit), and you also need to pay for dental and optical services. Registered students are covered for accidents, but should insure against loss or theft of personal items.

Higher education
Ireland has seven university colleges, 14 institutes of technology and a

number of specialist and private colleges. Degrees normally take between three and four years – the Bachelor qualification can be general, honours or special. UK nationals have the right to study in Ireland – although those thinking about full-time study should think about costs, travel and transferability of qualifications prior to enrolment. The most common way for UK students to study in Ireland is through an exchange.

History of accepting foreign students

There are good, wide-ranging opportunities for international students within exchange programmes and full-time study. Most courses are taught in English, although a small number are in Gaelic. Most institutions have an international office supported by student unions and other organisations, creating a positive environment for international/exchange students.

Fees

You will not normally pay fees if you are an EU citizen. Budget for €670 for annual registration, examination and student services costs.

Working while studying

You'll need to think carefully about funding your studies in Ireland, as it's difficult to finance yourself through part-time work. This may be available on a seasonal basis, especially in large cities and towns, although competition can be stiff.

Application system/visas

Exchange students should contact the international office at their own institution. Applications for full-time study are made through the Central Admissions Office (CAO) – the deadline for EU nationals is normally 1 February, although late applications can be made until 1 May (these can be done online, the CAO website has full details). You can choose up to ten degree courses, plus up to ten diploma or certificate courses on the application form, by order of preference.

UK nationals don't need a visa to live or study in Ireland.

Expenses/costs

The Irish Council for International Students estimates a minimum of €7,600 a year to cover living and entertainment costs. Dublin is more expensive.

Accommodation/assistance

Most higher education institutions in Ireland provide on-campus accommodation, but this is often quite expensive at around €190 monthly, and depending on the institution. For more information, see information sheet no. 11 on university residences, from the Irish Council for International Students, ICOS. There is also a good range of private accommodation.

Academic year

This is run in two semesters, from September–December and January–June.

Support network

All higher education institutions have student unions that are active in academic/cultural issues – these provide good information on enrolment, health and welfare matters, as well as a wide range of clubs and societies in sport, cultural and political activities.

Volume/type of work

This depends on your chosen subject but the format, structure and workload is similar to an English university, making Ireland worth considering as a study destination, whether full time or an exchange.

Useful addresses/websites

Central Admissions Office
Tower House
Eglington St
Galway
Republic of Ireland
Tel: (+353) 91 509800
Fax: (+353) 91 562344
Email: help@cao.ie
Websites: www.cao.ie
www.hei.ie

Irish Council for International Students (ICOS)
41 Morehampton Road
Donnybrook
Dublin 4
Republic of Ireland
Tel: (+353) 1 660 5233
Fax: (+353) 1 669 2320
Email: office@icosirl.ie
Website: www.icosirl.ie

Irish Embassy
17 Grosvenor House
London SW1X 7HR
Tel: 020 7235 2171
Fax: 020 7235 2851
Email: ir.embassy@lineone.net
Website: http://ireland.embassyhomepage.com

Case study 1
University College, Cork (UCC)

Background

Founded in 1845, and originally known as Queen's College, UCC is one of Ireland's oldest higher education institutions. Since 1997, it's been incorporated into the University of Ireland, and has a reputation as the country's leading research institute. Cork is noted for its magnificent coastline and is an excellent base to explore the West of Ireland.

Structure

Eight faculties (including arts, Celtic studies and science) with 14,500 students, of which there are more than 1,000 international students from over 60 countries. There's an extensive support system to assist international/exchange students.

Social life

Cork is a lively place to study – there are over 100 clubs and societies, covering political, artistic and sporting interests. Cork City has many pubs, bars, eating places, cafes and cinemas and theatres.

Applications/accommodation

Exchange students should click on the Erasmus/Socrates link of the International Education Office website, and contact their home institution. For full-time study, applications can be made via the website. You can also contact the admissions office for information about courses prior to application through the CAO.

The accommodation office can help you with information about living in Cork, whether in halls or off-campus private rentals. A student accommodation handbook is available on request.

Contact

International Education Office
West Wing
University College, Cork
Western Road
Cork
Republic of Ireland
Tel: (+353) 21 490 2543
Fax: (+353) 21 490 3118
Email: isoffice@ucc.ie
Website: www.ucc.ie

Case study 2
Institute of Technology, Tralee (ITT)

Background
Established in 1977, the Institute is an autonomous establishment at university level providing academic and vocational courses that serve market needs with strong links to industry and commerce. Tralee town is surrounded by some of the most beautiful countryside in Ireland.

Structure
ITT has only 3,500 students, giving it a friendly and supportive environment with good pastoral assistance. It offers courses in business, humanities, hotel and catering, engineering, science and computing. The international office provides a range of opportunities for study.

Social life
Though the town's winding streets can be wet and windswept at times, its pubs always have a welcoming atmosphere. If you don't like big city living, but prefer to be in a small community close to wonderful scenery, then Tralee could be the place for you. The Student Union and clubs will help to give you a flavour of Irish life.

Applications/accommodation
For exchanges, refer to the Erasmus/Socrates link, then check with your home institution. For information on full-time study, click on the courses link on the ITT's website, and apply through the CAO. There's a variety of good student accommodation in Tralee, from apartments to houses, hostels or family-share, depending whether your stay is short or long-term (you can find out more about this from the international office).

Contact
Institute of Technology, Tralee
Clash
Tralee
County Kerry
Republic of Ireland
Tel: (+353) 66 714 5600
Fax: (+353) 66 712 5711
Website: www.ittralee.ie

International Erasmus/Socrates Office
Institute of Technology, Tralee
Drumtacken
Tralee
County Kerry
Republic of Ireland
Tel: (+353) 66 714 5612
Fax: (+353) 66 714 5647
Email: info@tralee.ie
Website: www.ittralee.ie

Country profile: Italy

Population
57.9 million. The capital, Rome, has a population of 2.7 million.

History/government
Italy has been a republic since the end of the Second World War and was a founder member of the EEC in 1957. Italy has a coalition system, so that government is made up of two or more political parties. Italian politics is complex, with frequent elections and changes of government.

Culture, language and lifestyle
There is a long cultural tradition for music and the arts, dating back to the Renaissance and beyond – cultural centres include Florence, Rome and Venice, though there are many smaller places (Siena and Assisi, for example). The official language is Italian and 98 per cent of the population is Roman Catholic. The food reflects the country's regional diversity, with regions having their own types of pasta, wine and ice-cream. Lifestyle emphasizes eating and drinking well, and varies between the south and the north. In the south the lifestyle is shaped by the climate and the siesta is the norm. It is also poorer than the industrial north, which is more diverse and urban. Syle in fashion and cuisine are important.

Banking system/currency
The euro (€). Bank opening times are Monday–Friday, 8.30am–4.30pm (these can vary, particularly in the south), and there are extensive ATM facilities.

Climate/geography
Italy's climate is diverse. The south has hot, dry summers and mild winters, whereas in the northern Alps winters can be severe and the summers cool. The country also has a varied coastline.

Transport
A good rail network links all major towns and cities, and there are several types of train – check in advance of travel and reserve, if you're planning a long trip. There's also an extensive range of bus/coach travel on a national and regional basis.

Health arrangements
Take an E111 with you, and always consider insurance. You'll still have to pay a fee for treatment, together with part of the cost of any prescribed medicines. If you're going on exchange, the international office at your home institution will advise you on medical arrangements and insurance.

Higher education

There are 39 state universities, and a small number of private ones. Universities generally offer the full range of studies, although technical universities usually specialise in engineering and related disciplines, while university institutes generally focus on one area of learning.

The first degree is the *Laura* (4–6 years) although recently some institutions, especially private universities in Milan and Rome, have introduced the *Laura Brevi* (three years). Be sure to check the duration of bachelor programmes at the institutions that interest you.

History of accepting foreign students

UK students can study full-time courses in Italy – although the most common way is through the Erasmus/Socrates programme. All courses and lectures are given in Italian, so you need to have a good knowledge of the language – and to be accepted for full-time study you have to pass a proficiency test. Even if you're going on exchange, it's best to learn some Italian before going (most Italian universities provide language courses for foreigners). Think carefully about the language factor and check with your international office – Italian universities generally have well-developed links with UK universities.

Fees

Generally, you'll have to pay registration fees – these vary by course and institution, and can range from €170–230 a year. There are limited scholarships for study and research (you can get more information on this from the Italian Cultural Institute).

Working while studying

It's sometimes possible to find part-time work, especially in the larger cities and tourist centres but unemployment is high, particularly in the south. A good command of Italian is needed for most jobs.

Application system/visas

For full-time study, applications should be sent direct to the individual institution by the end of February for entry in the same year. Applicants need to show proof of residency and financial support. UK nationals don't require a visa to study, but do need a residence permit to stay for more than three months (this can be renewed each year). You can get further information on this from the Italian Embassy.

Expenses/costs

This can vary according to lifestyle and location, but it's best to budget around €413–516 monthly for food and accommodation.

Accommodation/assistance

Most universities have halls of residence (approx €154 monthly), but it's difficult for foreign students to get places. Most overseas students live in private accommodation – the availability, range and cost vary from region to region (allow €129–258 monthly for this). If you're going on exchange, check the arrangements that are in place between your home and partner institutions before arriving in Italy.

Academic year

This runs in two semesters, October/November to February/March, and February/March to June.

Support network

Most universities have good social and recreational facilities. They might also have an association offering general advice, especially during your settling-in period. Check with the Erasmus or international office for details.

Volume/type of work

Studying in Italy is a different challenge to the UK, as universities mostly have a long tradition of research and academic study – this varies by subject area. You'll need to be adaptable, as lectures are given for up to 500 students at times, and you may have only limited contact with professors. You will also be expected to follow up lectures with reading and independent study. Assessment is usually by examination (frequently oral and in public) with some coursework.

Useful addresses/websites

Italian Consulate
38 Eaton Place
London SW1X 8AN
Tel: 020 7235 9371
Fax: 0207 823 1809

Italian Cultural Institute
39 Belgrave Square
London SW1X 8WX
Tel: 020 7235 1461
Fax: 020 7235 4618
Email: ici@italcultur.org.uk
Website: www.italcultur.org.uk

Italian Embassy
14 Three Kings' Yard
London W1K 43H
Tel: 020 7312 2200

Fax: 020 7499 2283
Email: emblondon@embitaly.org.uk
Website: www.embitaly.org.uk/index/html

Ministry of Education
Viale Trastevere 76A
00153 Rome
Italy
Tel: (+39) 06 584 93620
Fax: (+39) 06 584 93619
Website: www.isstruzione.it/welcome.host.html

Case study 1
Università degli studi di Firenze (University of Florence)

Background
The university's history can be traced back as far as 1321, although its modern era dates from 1923. Based in the historic centre of Florence, it's within walking distance of the main train station, although its faculties are spread across the city – about 20 minutes away by bus.

Structure
Florence has 12 faculties, and approximately 60,000 students – full-time students can enrol for three-year degrees. Each faculty has a website which you can consult for details of specific courses. There is an international office to help international/exchange students, and each faculty also has an international coordinator to help with more specific enquiries – these should be your initial point of contact. There are also Italian language courses for foreigners available.

Social life
Florence is a fascinating place in which to live and study, with monuments, theatres, churches, museums and many cinemas, clubs, bars and restaurants throughout the narrow streets and large squares. The Cultural Centre for Foreigners (www.unifi.it/unifi/ccs) is a good starting point. However, Florence can be expensive – the international office estimates that you'll need about €550 monthly to cover basic living costs.

Applications/accommodation
For exchange students, application/enrolment forms must be

received by the appropriate faculty at least 45 days in advance of arrival in Florence – your home institution can advise you about procedure, although you should follow all the steps laid down by the university carefully. If you're interested in full-time study, contact the relevant faculty (use the website in English to find details of this) and then go through the admissions office.

The university doesn't offer any direct help with accommodation, and it can be difficult to find a place to live, especially in or near the city centre. You're advised to visit in advance to find accommodation, especially if you're planning to study full-time. The Azienda Regionale can help you, and there are hostels throughout the city offering short-term board while you look (the accommodation link on the university website gives useful tips and advice).

Contact
Hacienda Requite per il Diretto allo Studio Università di Firenze
Viale Gramsci 36–38
50121 Firenze
Italy
Tel: (+39) 55 305 522611
Email: mbox@azistu.fi.it
Website: www.azistu.fi.it

Universita degli studi di Firenze
Ufficio Orientamento Mobilita Collaborazioni Studentesche
Piazza San Marco 4
50121 Firenze
Italy
Tel: (+39) 55 275 7671
Fax: (+39) 55 275 7681
Email: arrivals@adm.unifi.it
Website: www.unifi.it

Country profile: Latvia

Population
2.5 million. The capital, Riga, has a population of 840,000.

History/government
Latvia first became independent in 1918, but in 1940 it was absorbed into the Soviet Union, until 1991. It is set to join the EU in May 2004.

Culture, language and lifestyle
Latvia has been strongly influenced by progress towards independence, and is now shaking off its Soviet legacy. The official language is Latvian, although 30 per cent of the population still speak Russian. Latvian food is consistent with its neighbours – good solid meat, fish, potatoes and vegetables, and fast food outlets are increasing. Latvia is a young country, both in terms of its independence and the age of the population. Much of the social life centres on bars, with good, inexpensive local beer, though eating and drinking in Riga can seem expensive.

Banking system/currency
The lat (Ls), although this will change to the euro (€) some time after Latvia joins the EU in 2004. Bank opening hours vary, but in Riga they are generally 10am–5pm.

Climate/geography
The Baltic Sea gives the country a maritime climate, with July as the warmest month. It's generally damp and mild. There's plenty of unspoilt coastline and inland forests.

Transport
Internal transport is reasonable as the country is small. Major airlines fly to Riga and there's a useful (if sometimes slow) train network. Latvia can be reached by sea from Denmark and Sweden.

Health arrangements
There are no reciprocal arrangements with the UK, so you must have insurance cover. Foreign residents often use private healthcare clinics, as these have higher standards.

Lifestyle

Higher education
There are five universities and a number of specialised higher education colleges, falling into two types of institution: academic and professional. Bachelor's degrees usually last four years, although there is a three-year

bridging arrangement before a decision is taken on the final direction (whether academic – *Magistrs* – or professional).

History of accepting foreign students
Latvia has only been part of Erasmus since 1997, so exchange programmes are still developing (and the UK isn't well represented yet). Increasing numbers of students are going to Latvia from areas such as China and India, and courses taught in English are beginning to appear.

Fees
First degrees cost around US$3,000 a year.

Application system/visas
Exchange students should apply via their home institution. For full-time study, there's no centralised system, so you need to apply direct to the university. Entrance is competitive and through exams, with international candidates and with Latvian nationals both applying for places. Entrance requirements can be checked through the Latvian Academic Information Centre (www.aic.lv), and websites for Latvian universities can be accessed via www.piapa.lv.

British students do not need a visa for studying in Latvia, just an up-to-date UK passport.

Expenses/costs
Housing costs up to US$80 monthly and living (food, transport, etc) about US$250 monthly. Acute health insurance is about US$15 monthly.

Accommodation/assistance
Most universities have dormitory-style halls, but spaces are very limited. Private accommodation is quite cheap but can be difficult to find.

Support network
Student unions organise clubs and other social activities.

Volume/type of work
The Latvian educational system is based to some extent on the Germanic model, so workloads can seem heavy with an expectation of independent learning; teaching is mainly done in large group lectures. Each stage of work can be assessed via a thesis.

Useful addresses/websites
Embassy of Latvia
45 Nottingham Place
London W1U 5LR
Tel: 020 7312 0040
Email: embassy@embassyoflatvia.co.uk

Latvian Academic Information Centre
Valnu iela 2
Riga LV 1098
Latvia
Tel: (+371) 722 5155
Fax: (+371) 721 2317
Website: www.aic.lv

Case study
Riga Technical University

Background
Riga's university was founded in 1862, and is one of the first technical higher education institutions in north-east Europe. It was based on Swiss and German models, and now has around 13,000 students.

Structure
There are English-language programmes in the following faculties: civil engineering, computer science and IT, electronics and communications, engineering, economics, transport and mechanical engineering and business studies. The university is establishing links internationally and through Erasmus. There are six facilities including a Business Institute.

Social life
There's a well equipped sports complex on campus and the city of Riga offers a good range of social activities.

Applications/accommodation
There are no study grants or scholarships offered by the university. Apply direct via the university's International Relations Unit, or through your home institution for exchanges. For accommodation, the university has dormitory-type halls, but places are limited.

Full-time applicants need to obtain an invitation to study, issued by the university, and a Latvian visa. For more information go to www.rtuasd.lv.

Contact
International Relations Unit
Riga Technical University
Kalku 1
Riga LV1050

Latvia
Tel: (+371) 708 9313
Fax: (+371) 708 9020
Email: igors@latnet.lv
Website: www.rtuasd.lv

Country profile: Lithuania

Population
3.5 million. The capital, Vilnius, has a population of 543,000.

History/government
Lithuania's history is marked by periods of independence and foreign occupation, most notably by Russia in the 19th century, USSR and Nazi Germany in the 1940s, and lastly the Soviet Union. Lithuania became independent in 1991. In 2003, 91 per cent of Lithuanians voted to join the EU in 2004.

Culture, language and lifestyle
Lithuanian is the official language. The majority of the population is Lithuanian (80 per cent) and Roman Catholic. Due to the country's favourable coastal position, and that 40 per cent of the land is devoted to agriculture, Lithuania is well supplied with a wide variety of fresh produce including meat, fish, grains and dairy products. The lifestyle depends on where you choose to live. The society as a whole is emerging from relative isolation.

Banking system/currency
The Lithuanian litas (Lt). This will change to the euro (€) after Lithuania joins the EU in May 2004. Banking hours are Monday–Friday, from 9am–5pm, although some banks also open on Saturday from 9am–1pm.

Climate/geography
Mostly flat country, with much farmland and forests and a large number of lakes and rivers. Vilnius is surrounded on three sides by wooded hills and is situated in a picturesque river valley. Summer is warm, spring and autumn are relatively mild and winter (November to mid-March) can be very cold. The heaviest rain falls in August, and heavy snowfalls are common in winter.

Transport
The national airline, Lithuanian Airlines (TE), flies to several European capitals. There's a well-developed rail network, with Vilnius as the focal point, and ferry services to Denmark, Germany and Sweden from Klaipeda.

Health arrangements
The UK has no reciprocal health agreement with Lithuania, so you need to take out medical insurance. Emergency treatment for foreign tourists is free, but all other medical services have to be paid. The standard of

state care is below that of the UK; resident foreigners usually opt for treatment in private clinics.

History of accepting foreign students
Lithuania has 35 higher education institutions, including 19 universities and 16 colleges with around 120,000 students – 60 per cent are enrolled on bachelor degree courses (*Bakalauras*, usually taking 4–5 years).

Teaching is in Lithuanian, although some instruction is available in English, German or Russian. If you're considering an exchange, you should check with your home institution as to which courses are offered in English. If you're contemplating full-time study, check with the university direct, and be prepared to learn Lithuanian.

Fees
Foreign students are charged tuition fees varying between US$1,300–3,000 a year. The amount is set by the individual institutions and includes the cost of using libraries, laboratories, medical services and, sometimes, accommodation.

Working while studying
There are no restrictions for citizens of the EU to work in Lithuania, but it's advisable to confirm this before taking paid employment.

Application system/visas
Contact the institution directly at least three months before the start of the course (the academic year commences in September), as each has a slightly different method of application. You can only get a student visa when you've been offered a place to study.

All visitors require a valid passport with at least one year's validity. If you're planning to study in Lithuania for more than three months, you'll need to get a temporary residence permit (valid for up to one year).

Expenses/costs
Students in Lithuania must meet all costs, including their own tuition, unless these are met by an exchange programme such as Erasmus/ Socrates. There are some state scholarships available for foreign students to help with fees and basic living costs. Budget for around 1,000 Lt (£220) monthly.

Accommodation/assistance
A range of accommodation is available, from rooms in dormitories at 100 Lt a month, to rooms in private homes and self-contained apartments at 500 Lt a month and upwards. Accommodation is usually arranged via the institution's international relations office or the student union.

Academic year
This runs in two semesters, from September–January and February–June.

Support network
Your main point of contact is the international office. There are a range of clubs and associations at most universities which you can join. Although the universities are developing their international profile, you'll need to be flexible, adaptable and independent to fully benefit from study in Lithuania.

Volume/type of work
The volume of studies is measured by credits (one credit = 40 hours in classes, laboratories, etc), or by one working week. Depending on study content and qualifications, all consecutive programmes are divided into six study areas: arts, humanities, social, physical, biomedical and technological sciences. Undergraduate study programmes consist of three groups of subjects: fundamental disciplines, the basics of the study programme and special training.

Teaching consists of lectures, seminars and group work. Independent study is very important.

Useful addresses/websites
Embassy of Lithuania
84 Gloucester Place
London W1U 6AU
Tel: 020 7486 6401
Fax 020 7486 6403
Website: www.users.globalnet.co-uk/-Iralon/

Ministry of Education and Science
A Volano G 2/7
Vilnius 2600
Lithuania
Tel: (+370) 274 3125
Email: smmin@smm.lt
Website: www.smm.lt

Case Study
Universitas Vilnensis (University of Vilnius)

Background
Founded in 1579 and located in the heart of the country's capital, the university is one of the oldest in eastern and central Europe.

Structure

Vilnius has twelve faculties, eight institutes, ten study and research centres, the oldest library in Lithuania, a university hospital, astronomical observatory, botanic garden, computer centre and St John's Church. In 2003, Vilnius had 1,219 academic staff, 170 professors and 21,284 students. In 2003–4, 185 courses were offered in foreign languages, of which over 90 per cent were in English.

Social life

Along with the usual array of cosmopolitan attractions, cafes, bars, galleries, theatres, festivals and modern shops, Vilnius is a city that can be enjoyed round the clock. Travel within the city is cheap and easy using the bus network, while international transport is provided by local rail and air links.

Applications/accommodation

Good command of Lithuanian doesn't apply for exchange and non-degree students. Application for full-time study should be made directly to the university. For exchanges you should initially contact the international office of your home university to see if bilateral arrangements exist.

Overseas students can stay at either one of the student residences or rent a flat in the city. Rates for student accommodation range from 220 Lt (sharing a room) to 320 Lt (single occupancy) a month. A deposit of around 400 Lt is usually required. The price for a one or two-room flat in the city starts at around 700 Lt per month. Both types of accommodation can be arranged via the International Programme and Relations Office.

Contact

International Programme and Relations Office
University of Vilnius
Universiteto St. 3
Vilnius 2734
Lithuania
Tel: (+370) 5 268 7049
email: trs@cr.vu.lt
Website: http://www.vu.lt

Country profile: the Netherlands

Population
16 million. The capital, Amsterdam, has a population of 1.1 million.

History/government
The Netherlands is a constitutional monarchy. The queen is the head of state and the prime minister the head of government.

Culture, language and lifestyle
A modern, progressive country, home to famous orchestras and arts events. Its cultural heritage brings people from around the world to visit its museums and galleries, as well as to admire the architecture and canals. Traditional Dutch food is simple and healthy, based on good ingredients cooked simply. Breakfast includes bread, cold meat and cheese. Another important aspect of Dutch cuisine is Indonesian food. Dutch is one of the two official languages and used by most people. Frisian is spoken by around 0.5 million people in Friesland.

The large cities are interesting and lively places. Population density is high but the countryside is popular for leisure activities such as cycling, walking or fishing. Hard work and punctuality are valued.

Banking system/currency
The euro (€). The banking system is similar to the UK's, although cheques are used less frequently. Many UK banks also operate there. Banking hours are generally from Monday–Friday, 9am–4pm, and plenty of ATMs are available.

Climate/geography
The Netherlands is very flat with much of the coast below sea level, protected by dunes and dykes. The major rivers forming the delta on which the Netherlands is located are the Rhine, Waal, Lek, Maas and Schelde. There are just a few hills in the south and east. The winters are generally mild with a fair amount of rain, although there can be bitterly cold periods when the canals freeze. Summers are warm.

Transport
The main airport is Amsterdam Schiphol. There is a very efficient rail system with some high-speed trains. The road network is also good, with over 1,200 miles of motorway. Bicycles are used regularly (there are 1,000kms of cycle paths). Students are subsidised on much of the public transport.

Health arrangements
All Dutch residents must have health insurance, whether private or

public. Before you can study you must take out your own health and liability insurance.

Higher education

University and professional education are the main types of higher education. While research-oriented university courses cover the traditional academic areas, courses at higher professional institutions (HBOs) are practical, preparing students for careers. Courses last for four years and both offer degrees. The international dimension is important in all types of higher education.

History of accepting foreign students

Dutch universities have always welcomed foreign students.

Fees

All students have to pay €1,400, although EU students may be entitled to some restitution.

Working while studying

There are no restrictions on working while studying, and a work permit isn't required. There are special websites for students looking for work – check with the student union.

Application system/visas

For exchanges, contact your own institution. There is a central application system, but if you're an independent foreign student planning to study full-time, you need to contact the institution direct. Visas aren't required for UK students, but if you stay for over three months a residence permit is needed.

Expenses/costs

You'll need to budget for about €14,000 annually, taking in the cost of registration and tuition fees, insurance, student union membership and general living expenses. This can vary according to area.

Accommodation/assistance

Student housing is in short supply. There are few halls of residence and most students rent flats or take rooms in private households. However, universities will do all they can to help exchange students, either arranging accommodation or providing lists of approved addresses. Each institution has a student housing service that keeps a register of accommodation.

Academic year

The academic year runs in two semesters, September–January and February–June.

Support network
Student unions provide support, as does the Foreign Student Service (FSS). There are also counsellors and mentors in most institutions.

Volume/type of work
This depends on the type of institution, whether traditional/academic or vocational. Programmes usually require around 40 hours of study a week, including contact time and private study.

The most common form of teaching is the seminar or working group. A large portion of all study programmes is spent working in groups to analyse and solve problems under a tutor's supervision. Students in Dutch universities are expected to become independent learners with a critical attitude. In the HBOs active, practical work is required and there's little requirement for essay writing. Assessment is usually by written paper or exam and oral presentation.

Useful addresses/websites
Foreign Student Service (FSS)
Oranje Nassaulaan 5
1075 AH Amsterdam
The Netherlands
Tel: (+31) 020 671 5915
Fax: (+31) 20 676 0555
Email: info@unescocentrum.nl
Website: www.unescocentrum.nl

Nuffic (Netherlands Organisation for International Cooperation in Higher Education)
Kortenaerkade 11
PO Box 29777
2502 LT The Hague
The Netherlands
Tel: (+31) 70 42 60 260
Fax: (+31) 70 42 60 399
Email: nuffic@nuffic.nl or divis@nuffic.nl
Website: www.nuffic.nl

Royal Netherlands Embassy
38 Hyde Park Gate
London SW7 5DP
Tel: 020 7590 3200
Fax: 020 7225 0947
Email: cultural@netherlands-embassy.org.uk
Website: www.netherlands-embassy.org.uk

Case study 1
Universiteit van Amsterdam (University of Amsterdam)

Background
Became the Universiteit van Amsterdam in 1877. Rapid growth followed, with more fields of study being introduced and new departments established. Most faculties are still located at historic sites throughout the city centre.

Structure
The university has seven faculties covering humanities, social science, law, economics, medicine, dentistry and sciences. Around 22,000 students are enrolled, including 2,500 international students. Teaching is in Dutch but a number of English courses are offered. International schools and institutes, such as the Amsterdam Law School, have programmes taught in English. The university is committed to internationalisation.

Social life
Every department has its own student groups that organise social activities and represent student interests. The International Student Network (ISN) looks after the interests of foreign students, and the cultural organisation (CREA) organises courses and projects in drama, film and music, etc.

Applications/accommodation
For exchanges, your institution can advise you. For independent study, initially you should contact the Service and Information Centre. Applications from foreign students are made directly to the university.

Student housing is in very short supply and quite expensive. There are a few university residences, some quite far from the city centre. Other students live in apartments in older neighbourhoods. The university has signed an agreement with two housing corporations to provide furnished accommodation – university programme coordinators will apply for this. Otherwise, you're advised to start looking early and stay in a cheap hostel until you've found somewhere suitable.

Contact
Service and Information Centre
Universiteit van Amsterdam
Binnengasthuisstraat 9

1012 ZA Amsterdam
The Netherlands
Tel: (+31) 20 525 8080
Fax: (+31) 20 525 2921
Email: info@uva.nl
Website: www.english.uva.nl/education

Case study 2
Haagse Hogeschool (The Hague University of
Professional Education)

Background
Founded in 1987, Haagse Hogeschool is one of 56 institutions that
offer higher professional education in the Netherlands. The
hogescholen differ from universities in that they train students for
specific careers at an academic level. The university is located in
striking new buildings near the main Hollands Spoor rail station;
both the old city and Scheveningen (the port and lively beach
resort) are close by.

Structure
Haagse Hogeschool has more than 15,000 students, 27 full-time
and 24 part-time study programmes (some taught in English),
including the business-related HEBO programme (in which
students spend two semesters studying abroad and on a work
placement). In the third-year HEBO course, the places of students
abroad are filled by an international intake from HEBO's partners.

Social life
Many student activities – sports, drama and parties – are organised by the Student Union (HEBOS). Special events are arranged
for foreign students, including an introductory week before the
courses start, and clubs, bars and cafes make for a varied and
hectic social life.

Applications/accommodation
For exchanges, contact your own institution. Independent
students should get in touch with the Information Centre initially
for advice on courses and admissions. Applications go direct to the
Hogeschool.
    There is little student accommodation available, although

exchange students are given help in finding somewhere to live. Most students live in apartments or furnished rooms in private houses and flats, or at home. Information and an application form are sent when you are offered a place. The system is efficient but deadlines are tight, so pay close attention to any requirements.

Contact

Information Centre
Haagse Hogeschool
PO Box 13336
2501 EH The Hague
The Netherlands
Tel: (+31) 70 445 8585
Fax: (+31) 70 445 8825
Email: info@hhs.nl
Website: www.sost.hhs.nl

Country profile: New Zealand

Population
3.7 million. The capital, Wellington, has a population of 920,000.

History/government
New Zealand was the last of the world's significant landmasses to be colonised by people. It is a nation of immigrants. The Maoris settled in the country less than 1,000 years ago while Europeans arrived just 350 years ago. Together these peoples have forged a unique identity.

Culture, language and lifestyle
New Zealand has an outdoor lifestyle that can be lively in towns and cities, but pretty quiet in the rural areas. Food is good, with meals based around meat. English is widely spoken, and there is a strong Maori culture.

New Zealanders enjoy an outdoor lifestyle, although things can appear quite quiet outside of the main towns.

Banking system/currency
New Zealand dollar (NZ$). The banking system is similar to the UK's. Banks are open 9.30am–4.30pm, Mon–Fri.

Climate/geography
The country consists of two large islands, North and South. The north is more densely populated and has a generally milder climate that can be sub-tropical. South Island is more mountainous and wetter.

Transport
Generally good standard rail and road connections. Internal flights play a very useful and cost-effective role.

Health arrangements
There is a reciprocal healthcare agreement, so UK nationals have the same arrangements as New Zealanders. But this still means that some services have to be paid for, and you must have insurance.

Higher education
This is very similar to the UK system, with seven universities and 25 polytechnics. Bachelor degrees usually take three years, but can last up to six. The best source of information is the Association of Commonwealth Universities (ACU).

History of accepting foreign students
There is much in New Zealand's favour, including teaching in English

and a generally welcoming atmosphere. However, the differential fees structure (see below) is a disincentive. There may be a very limited number of partial scholarships available from ACU. Higher education tends to target students from the Pacific Rim and South-East Asia.

Fees
Overseas students pay more than New Zealand nationals, between £3,000 and £6,000 a year, according to the course and subject.

Working while studying
If you are on a course of more than 12 months this is possible during the summer vacation as long as you get a different visa to the standard summer visa, which can be obtained from the local NZ Immigration Service on payment of a fee. It's likely that opportunities for part-time work will be very limited.

Application system/visas
Apply direct to the university as far in advance as possible. Enrolment is usually in February for the first semester, and in July for the second. You need to make enquiries at least six months beforehand. Successful applicants receive a pre-enrolment form in October or April which must be sent back to the university. Applications can also be made through a centralised form from Education New Zealand or the New Zealand High Commission (see below).

You'll also need to apply to the Immigration Service at the High Commission prior to entry, showing that you have a guarantee of accommodation and finance to support yourself while studying.

Expenses/costs
It's best to budget for around £3,500–4,000 a year for food, clothing, transport and entertainment (excluding accommodation).

Accommodation/assistance
Most institutions have halls/hostels costing around NZ$200 a week. Private rentals cost around NZ$120. There are also private hostels (NZ$120 a week) and homestay (NZ$180). Institutions provide accommodation lists. The Eucation New Zealand website (below) is very helpful.

Academic year
This runs in two semesters, January–May, and June–November.

Support network
University international offices help with enrolment, orientation, welfare and assist with accommodation, either in halls or private.

Volume and type of work
This is similar to the UK.

Useful addresses/websites
Education New Zealand
PO Box 10–500
Wellington
New Zealand
Tel: (+64) 4 472 0788
Fax: (+64) 4 471 2828
Email: enquiry@education.org.nz
Website: www.educationnz.org.nz

New Zealand High Commission
New Zealand House
80 Haymarket
London SW1Y 4TQ
Tel: 020 7930 8422
Fax: 020 7839 4580
Email: newzealand@newzealandhc.org.uk
Website: www.nzembassy/com/home/cfm/

Case study
Northlands Polytechnic

Background
A small and friendly institution based in New Zealand's northern-most city, Whangarei (pop. 45,000), about two hours from Auckland. The campus is five minutes from the centre in pleasant parkland. Whangarei enjoys a sub-tropical climate and is close to some of the best ocean beaches in the country, as well as the stunning Bay of Islands.

Structure
Offers Bachelor degrees in applied arts, business management, applied information systems and nursing, as well as courses at certificate and diploma level.

Social life
A great location for outdoor living and all forms of watersports, as well as a good range of other sports.

Applications/accommodation
Apply on the form (downloadable from the polytechnic website).

Fees for Bachelor degrees are NZ$14,500 per year, with a registration fee of NZ$135. The international centre can give you advice on a range of issues, including visa applications and insurance arrangements, as well as travel from Auckland. The polytechnic also offers homestay arrangements at NZ$150 per week.

Contact
Northlands Polytechnic
Raumanga Valley Road
Whangarei
New Zealand
Tel: (+64) 9 459 8775
Email: overseas@northland.ac.nz
Website: www.northland.ac.nz

Country profile: Norway

Population
4.5 million. The capital, Oslo, has a population of 0.72 million.

History/government
Norway is a constitutional monarchy with a parliament, the *Storting*, and the king as head of state.

Culture, language and lifestyle
The vast majority of the population speak Norwegian. Its culture was formed by its association with the sea, through fishing and boatbuilding. It's an industrial nation, as well as highly progressive: Norway was one of the first countries to eradicate illiteracy and to grant the vote to women. Norwegian authors, composers and artists are internationally famous. Norwegian food traditions are based on simple first-class raw materials. All fish and seafood are popular, and you'll find different varieties of game, moose, elk or reindeer. Sales of alcohol are restricted: the cheapest can be found at the state-controlled *Vinmonopolet*.

Outdoor activities are very important in Norway, from hiking and fishing to skiing, even in summer. Norway has sophisticated cities and a high standard of living, making it an expensive place to live. Social equality is important as in all Scandinavian countries. In this respect, education is central.

Banking system/currency
The Norwegian krone (Kr). Anyone planning to stay more than six months needs a Norwegian ID number in order to open a bank account. For students, this procedure can be organised at university. Banks will make special provisions if you are planning to stay less than six months. ATMs are widely available. Banks are open 8.15am–3pm, Mon–Fri, 5pm on Thursday.

Climate/geography
The coastline is rugged and deeply intersected by fjords. In winter there is plenty of snow and ice with the temperature ranging from –5C to –20C. Summer can be sunny, but the temperature can remain low (–10C to 25C).

Transport
Oslo is the main airport. The road system is good; in the west of the country some road journeys continue by ferry when interrupted by fjords. There are regular ferries and high-speed ships, and the Norwegian state railway (NSB) has a network that stretches as far as Bodo on the coast of Nordland. Student fares are subsidised.

Health arrangements

The health care system is comprehensive. All students registered at a university upon payment of the semester fee become members of the student welfare organisation and eligible for the national health insurance scheme. This pays for all medical consultation and hospital costs, but not dental and medication costs or costs for transportation home if needed. You should get insurance before you travel. All residents, including students, must choose a specific doctor or clinic for their GP.

Higher education

There are four universities and university colleges of arts and science offering first and second degrees lasting from four to seven years, as well as doctorates. There are also 26 state university colleges offering courses with a more vocational orientation.

History of accepting foreign students

The number of international students is growing with the increase in participation in exchange and mobility programmes. Previously the language barrier and length of courses have been a deterrent.

Fees

There are no tuition fees to pay in Norwegian universities.

Working while studying

Students from EU countries can work part-time up to 20 hours a week without a permit. There are usually careers offices on campus that can help you to find temporary work.

Application system/visas

Exchange students should contact their own institution first. Independent students who want to study full-time should apply direct to the institution by 1 February. EU students do not need a visa, but those staying for more than six months need to fill in a form of notification to the National Registry and apply for a residence permit.

Expenses/costs

The high cost of living in Norway makes it an expensive place to study. It is estimated that a minimum monthly expenditure of around Kr6,000 is necessary for accommodation, food, books and transport (a deposit is needed for housing). Don't forget the cost of appropriate clothing for the harsh winters and leisure. Fees are paid each semester to the student welfare organisation: this is around Kr400, but varies between universities.

Accommodation/assistance

All foreign students at Norwegian universities are guaranteed accommodation in a single room at a university hostel (run by student welfare organisations). A room can be reserved by returning your acceptance form, along with a deposit.

Academic year
This runs in two semesters: August–December and January–June.

Support network
The Student Welfare Organisations (SiB) provides social and academic support for all students. There are also services specifically set up for international students.

Volume/type of work
Lecture programmes aren't heavy, but students in Norway are expected to be self-motivated and to study independently. A variety of teaching methods are used: lectures, seminars, fieldwork or lab work. Students can be assessed by oral or written examination, or a thesis.

Useful addresses/websites
Norwegian Tourist Board
5th Floor, Charles House
5 Lower Regent Street
London SW1Y 4LR
Tel: 0906 302 2003
Fax: 020 7839 6993
Email: infouk@ntr.no
Website: www.visitnorway.com

Royal Norwegian Embassy
25 Belgrave Square
London SW1X 8QD
Tel: 020 7591 5500
Fax: 020 7245 6993
Email: emb.london@mfa.no
Website: www.norway.org.uk

UCAS Norway
Postboks 1133
Blindern
0317 Oslo
Norway
Tel: (+47) 22 85 88
Email: postmottak@so.uio.no

Case study
Universitet i Oslo (University of Oslo)

Background
Founded in 1811 as the Royal Frederick University when Norway was still under Danish rule, the University of Oslo is Norway's oldest and largest higher education institution. It has approximately 30,000 students, including around 400 international students.

Structure
Eight faculties: theology, law, medicine, arts, mathematics and natural sciences, dentistry, social sciences and education. Teaching for bachelor's degrees is in Norwegian.

Social life
The university offers an active social life. The international buddy system hooks up international students with a senior student who can help them to settle in. A special events programme is organised by SIO, and the International Students' Union represents the needs of international students. The Oslo Students Sports Club (OSI) is one of the largest in Norway, run by and for students with great facilities, including winter sports. City living in Oslo gives you plenty of social opportunities.

Applications/accommodation
Applications for places on exchange and mobility programmes should be sent via your own institution. Independent students' applications should be made direct to the university, and they need to get a copy of the *International Student Guide* 2004–5 (from the website) for details of specific courses. Admission to professional courses such as medicine is restricted. The International Office can give you advice on all of the above.

International students are allocated a single room in one of the student residences – to reserve a room, just return the acceptance form that's sent to you with the offer of a study place, along with a deposit.

Contact
International Office
University of Oslo
Boks 1072
Blindern
0316 Oslo

Norway
Tel: (+47) 22 85 50 50
Email: international@admin.uio.no
Website: www.uio.no

Country profile: Poland

Population
38.6 million. The capital, Warsaw, has a population of 1.65 million.

History/government
Following several centuries of war and conflict, Poland was partitioned between Russia, Austria and Prussia at the end of the 18th century. The Polish state was not re-established until 1918. The Second World War led to invasion by Germany and the Soviet Union. Communist rule continued for many years after the war, but Poland is now a parliamentary republic.

Culture, language and lifestyle
Poland offers a variety of cultural experiences. There are famous music festivals and outstanding art collections, and 20th-century drama, film and theatre are internationally renowned. Polish cuisine developed as a response to the harsh central European climate – traditional dishes are based on pork, cabbage and potatoes with sausages, and soups and stews are popular. The official language is Polish.

Poland is neither Slavonic nor Germanic in character but a little of both, with lots of flair and high spirits. The big cities are typical of central Europe with plenty of cafes, bars and restaurants, museums, galleries and great architecture. Outside urban areas, life tends to be slower.

Banking system/currency
The Polish zloty, but this will change to the euro (€) some time after Poland joins the EU in 2004. ATMs are widely available. Banks are open 7.15am–5pm weekdays, and in cities on Saturday 9am–12pm.

Climate/geography
Poland has land borders with seven countries in central Europe. To the north there is the Baltic Sea coast, hosting a stretch of sandy beaches that are popular with tourists. The large plains in the centre form the main agricultural region. There are extensive mountains in the south. Poland has a temperate climate and there can be frequent rain.

Transport
There are seven international airports in Poland. Trains are very convenient (express and inter-city services require reservations, but are worth the extra cost). Bus services are also useful for travel around the country. Students can obtain discounts for some transport.

Health arrangements

The country has a good public medical care system as well as a private sector. Foreign students are usually allowed to consult doctors at academic medical centres which offer a wide range of services, but they also need to take out insurance before leaving for Poland.

Higher education

There are many higher education institutions in Poland, apart from traditional universities where nearly 40 per cent of students are enrolled. Over 20 per cent attend technical universities. There are also specialised colleges and academies; undergraduate courses last between three and four years.

History of accepting foreign students

There's a tradition of welcoming foreign students.

Fees

No tuition fees are charged to Polish students. Most foreign students are charged fees which vary between universities. They can range from £1,500–3,500 depending on the type of course, plus a registration fee of around £125.

Working while studying

Students on a short stay visa (see below) are only allowed to work during the summer holidays, and not for more than three months.

Application system/visas

Exchange students who want to go on the Erasmus/Socrates programme should contact their home institution. Independent students should contact the institution direct. There are no uniform admission rules but you should have the appropriate qualifications for university entry in the UK. All students are required to satisfy the university on health grounds and that they have sufficient command of the Polish language.

You'll need to get a visa to study – apply to the Consular Section of the Polish Embassy. Visas are granted for a maximum period of six months, and all foreigners staying in Poland for longer need to get a temporary residence permit and card.

Expenses/costs

These vary according to the course and location. Rooms in halls range from 115–145 zloty a month. There's a registration fee and insurance to consider as well as books, food and transport, but cost of living is significantly lower than in the UK.

Accommodation/assistance

Finding suitable accommodation can be a problem. For Erasmus students, a room in a student hostel might be arranged but there are only limited places. Rooms are often shared. The alternative is a privately rented room or flat in the city where you are studying.

Academic year
This is run in two semesters, August–December and February–June.

Support network
The international relations office in the university where you are studying will always give you advice. The students also have self-governing organisations providing a range of activities and support.

Volume/type of work
This is generally heavy. Courses are traditional in nature, and to be awarded a degree, students must complete all programmes of study successfully, submit and defend a thesis, and pass a diploma examination.

Useful addresses/websites
Embassy of Poland
47 Portland Place
London W1N 4JH
Tel: 020 7580 4324
Fax: 020 7323 4018
Website: Home.btclick.com/polishembassy

Polish Cultural Institute
34 Portland Place
London W1B 1HQ
Tel: 0870 774 2900
Fax: 020 7637 2190
Email: pci@polishculture.org.uk
Website: www.polishculture.org

Case study
Uniwersytet Jagiellonski w Krakowie
(Jagiellonian University Krakow)

Background
Founded in 1364 when Krakow was the royal capital, Jagiellonian is the oldest university in Poland. The partitioning of Poland at the beginning of the Second World War closed the university and many of the staff were sent to concentration camps. Not until the war was over and political repression had ended did the university

flourish again. It's located around the city with many buildings in the beautiful old town, while a new campus is under construction only 4kms from the city.

Structure

Thirteen faculties with over 20,400 students. The Study Abroad programme at the Centre for European Studies attracts many foreign students. Teaching is mainly in Polish, but there's a new undergraduate programme delivered in English: the Inter-disciplinary Programme in Humanities and Social Sciences. Intensive Polish language courses are provided throughout the year.

Social life

There's an active social life both on campus and in the old city, with its numerous clubs and cafes. The university has its own cinema, radio station and magazine. There are many other higher education institutions in Kraków, all contributing to the large student population and adding to the life of the city.

Applications/accommodation

Potential exchange students should apply to their home institu-tion. Independent students should contact the International Relations Office to talk about different faculties' requirements. It's possible that you'll have to take a competitive examination as well as satisfying UK university entrance requirements, and you must be able to show proficiency in Polish.

Limited places are available in student hostels, and there are very few single rooms. Many students rent furnished flats in the city centre. To have the chance of getting accommodation, applica-tion should be made before 15 June.

Contact

International Relations Office
Jagiellonian University Krakow
Ul.Golebia 24
31-007 Krakow
Poland
Tel: (+48) 12 422 1033 (ext.1105/1106)
Fax: (+48) 12 422 3229
Email: otrenska@adm.edu.pl
Website: www.uj.edu.pl

Country profile: Portugal

Population
10.2 million. The capital, Lisbon, has a population of 2.6 million.

History/government
A parliamentary democracy since the 1974 revolution. Portugal joined the EEC (now EU) in 1986.

Culture, language and lifestyle
Of the population, 64 per cent lives rurally, and 92 per cent is Catholic. The coastal regions are expanding, but inland rural areas are in decline. There is a strong festival culture; food is excellent and cheap, its Mediterranean influence mixes with the Atlantic. The emphasis is on a laid-back mediterranean lifestyle in the south, in contrast to the north where Germanic and Celtic influences are more prominent.

Banking system/currency
The euro (€). Banking hours are from 8.30am–3pm, weekdays. ATMs are widely available.

Climate/geography
The long Atlantic coast is Portugal's defining feature. It's quite mountainous in the north. Generally, it has a mild climate but with more rain in the north and it's often cooler, especially in the mountains.

Transport
The road system is getting better; the new Vasco de Gama bridge links Lisbon to the motorway network. There's a small and efficient train network. The bus journey from Lisbon airport to the city only takes 20 minutes.

Health arrangements
You should consider getting health insurance, and take form E111 with you. Some universities have their own healthcare facilities; pharmacists are highly trained and can dispense many drugs without prescription.

Higher education
There are both public and private institutions and universities, as well as more vocationally directed polytechnics. First degrees take between four and six years, leading to the *licenciado* although polytechnics offer a *bacharel* diploma after three years.

History of accepting foreign students
Portugal is a member of Erasmus, so there are plenty of exchange oppor-

tunities. As most courses are taught in Portuguese, places are limited to those students with an understanding of the language. Most universities involved in exchanges organise a Portuguese language training programme.

Fees
These will be a minimum of €300 per semester.

Application system/visas
Exchange students should apply through their home institution. International students are treated in the same way as Portuguese students; you need to apply direct to the institution. This is normally done in the first two weeks of August, as you may have to sit the first round of national admission examinations. There is a clearing process in October, when students can apply for places that are left over after the first round.

Once you arrive in Portugal you should apply for a residence permit from the local police. You will need evidence that you can support yourself financially. More information about procedures can be obtained from the Portuguese Embassy.

Expenses/costs
It's best to budget for €550 monthly to cover all costs except study materials, tuition and registration fees.

Accommodation/assistance
Cheaper than the UK, but there's very limited availability of halls (these cost €270 a month). You need to have a local address before you can get permission to stay in Portugal, so it's essential that you have accommodation arranged before you leave the UK.

Academic year
September/October–January, February–July.

Support network
This is generally quite heavy, working through international offices and student groups. Some universities have their own student welfare departments.

Type/volume of work
Study is quite formal in style; there is a good workload. You'll be expected to do a fair amount of independent study.

Useful addresses/websites
Portuguese Embassy
11 Belgrave Square

London SW1X 8PP
Tel: 020 7235 5331
Fax: 020 7445 1287
Email: portembassy-london@dialin.net
Website: www.portembassy.gla.ac.uk

Case study
Universidade de Lisboa (University of Lisbon)

Background

Founded in the late 18th century, Lisbon now has about 20,000 students. It's now one of the best-known Portuguese universities. Lisbon, spread over seven hills, is a charming, easy-going and immediately attractive city.

Structure

Faculties of science, letters, law, medicine, pharmacy, psychology and education, dentistry and fine arts. There are Erasmus coordinators in each faculty (see www.ul.pt/socrates/socrates for up-to-date information).

Social life

The university has a well-equipped sports centre, but the focus for social life is on the excellent facilities in and around the city. These range from excellent bars and good, cheap restaurants through to beaches at the nearby Costa de Caparica.

Applications/accommodation

Exchange students should go through their home institution initially. Independent students should contact the university direct as early as possible because of the selection process (see above). Free Portuguese language courses take place in October and February. To register, you need your passport, E111 and recent photos (plus a letter from your exchange coordinator, if appropriate).

The international relations office provides information on accommodation on request. The university has 12 student residences, and exchange students should apply via their faculty coordinator. Places for visiting students are very limited, and so you should apply as early as possible. The university has a social services department which helps with accommodation, meals (there are subsidised restaurants) and health. You need to obtain a social service card to take advantage of these benefits.

Contact
University of Lisbon
The following contacts are for the International Relations Office –
the university is highly devolved and each section has a different
address (see website for further details)
Tel: (+35) 12 17 963 759
Fax: (+35) 12 17 933 624
Email: gric@reitoria.ul.pt
Websites: www.ul.pt/ (in Portuguese)
www.ul.pt/socrates/socrates

Country profile: Romania

Population
22.6 million. The capital, Bucharest, has a population of 1.5 million.

History/government
Romanians trace themselves back to the Romans and the country blends this with its Balkan character. The country is slowly emerging from the Ceausescu regime, and is beginning to recover from virtual bankruptcy.

Culture, language and lifestyle
A polyglot culture with elements spanning Hungarians, Serbs, Ukrainians, Jews, Germans, Bulgarians, Turks and gypsies as well as ethnic Romanians. The official language is Romanian. The cuisine shows varying influences – at one level it's Balkan, then German and sometimes almost Mediterranean. Beers are good and there are some interesting local wines. Try Romanian doughnuts (*gogosi*).

Friendly and relaxed, if a bit anarchic. There is some focus on drinking in beer gardens and cellars as well as a growing number of bars and cafes. Nightclubs in Bucharest attract many students and other cities have lively student quarters. There are good winter sport facilities in the Carpathian mountains and excellent beach resorts along the Black Sea.

Banking system/currency
The Romanian lei. For changing money, use bureaux de change rather than banks for a better rate. ATMs are available in cities. It is probably better to exchange money at a private exchange bureau rather than bank, as the rate is usually better.

Climate/geography
Parts of the country are spectacular, especially the mountains of Transylvania. It's very hot and pleasant in the summer, and some areas can be cold in the winter (there are ski resorts in the mountains).

Transport
Cheap, if at times slow, trains and buses. Taxis in cities are cheap although you should agree a price at the start of your journey to avoid being overcharged.

Health arrangements
You'll need to take out medical insurance. UK nationals need a passport to get free medical treatment (this includes hospital and other medical treatments, plus some dental treatment). The best hospitals in

Bucharest are up to Western standards. You have to pay for medicines at a pharmacy.

Higher education
This particular sector has undergone swift growth, and there are now 133 universities – 49 state and 84 private – although many of these are specialist institutions. There have been measures to harmonise with the ECTS system and Romanian universities are members of the Erasmus exchange scheme.

History of accepting foreign students
Increasing interest has been stimulated by Erasmus membership, and courses are now being offered in English, French, German and Hungarian, as well as Romanian. There are a growing number of Erasmus links between Romanian and UK universities. The main university websites are available in English.

Fees
These are between £250 and £600 monthly.

Working while studying
Regulations for foreign workers in Romania are complex; this isn't a choice that should be relied on to fund your studies.

Application system/visas
Erasmus exchange students should check requirements with their home institution. Applications for international students are handled via the Ministry of National Education and Research (General Department of International Relations), and you can get forms from the Romanian Embassy. Checks are made into the student's medical history and academic record.

An entry visa can be obtained from the Romanian Embassy for stays of 30 days (cost is around £60. Please contact the embassy for full details), and after this, arrangements depend on the nature of the course (your university can advise you on this).

Expenses/costs
Romania is relatively cheap, although accommodation and eating out may seem quite expensive.

Accommodation/assistance
There is only limited halls accommodation, although overseas students often have a short period in halls whilst they organise more permanent private accommodation.

Academic year
September–January, February–June.

Support network
All universities have welfare organisations and, in most cases, there are special foreign student associations.

Volume/type of work
The work may seem quite academic and formal, and the volume is usually quite high.

Useful addresses/websites
Ministry of National Education and Research
General Department of International Relations
28–30 Gral Berthelot Street
Sect–1
70738 Bucharest
Romania
Tel: (+40) 21 312 1013
Fax: (+40) 21 315 7430
Website: www.edu.ro

Romanian Embassy
Arundel House
4 Palace Green
London W8 4QD
Tel: 020 7937 9666
Fax: 020 7937 8069
Email: postmaster-romania@embassyhomepage.com
Website: www.roemb.co.uk

Case study
Universitatea din Bucuresti
(University of Bucharest)

Background
The capital's leading university and one of the country's top higher education institutions with excellent research profiles, notably in the sciences. Bucharest has more than 100 bilateral agreements with other international universities. The city can be quite difficult to get to know, but it's well worth it.

Structure
The university has over 50 institutions, departments and research centres, including some outside the city. The university provides Romanian language programmes for international students, but also offers courses in English and other languages (contact the university for details as programmes are changing).

Social life
Bucharest has a lively nightlife and there are good arrangements for students on campus.

Applications/accommodation
Exchange students should go through their home institution. Full-time students should go through the Ministry of National Education and Research (see above). Exchange students are given priority for a room in the university guesthouse for the first ten days, at US$10 nightly and during this time you will be given help to find permanent accommodation. Non-exchange students have the possibility of rooms in university hostels (a limited number) or based in the private sector.

Contact
University of Bucharest
Bdul M. Kogalniceanu nr. 36–46 sector 5
050107 Bucuresti
Romania
Tel: (+40) 21 307 7300
Fax: (+40) 21 313 1760
Website: www.unibuc.ro

Country Profile: Russia

Population
150 million. The capital, Moscow, has a population of 13 million.

History/government
Since the collapse of communism in the early 1990s, Russia has moved towards a more democratic political structure. Executive power is held by the president. The president appoints the cabinet (ministers of state) to run various government departments.

Culture, language and lifestyle
Russia has a deep-rooted cultural tradition – the arts reflect many aspects of Russian life and society. The majority of the population is native Russian (81 per cent), although there are many ethnic minorities. Religion wasn't officially recognised during the communist era – but there is a long tradition of Russian Orthodoxy. The official language is Russian. Its traditional cuisine consists of caviar, cold soups, steamed and pickled cabbage, potatoes and vodka. Today the diet is more varied, including fast food and a variety of ethnic dishes from the provinces.

Living in Russia, even in the big cities like Moscow and St Petersburg, presents many contrasts and challenges. The Russian lifestyle is changing significantly in the post-communist period but there is still a fusion of the 'old' world and the new.

Banking system/currency
The rouble. ATMs are widely available, and hard currency is in great demand – you should take care when exchanging currency to avoid the black market.

Climate/geography
Russia has an extremely varied climate: one-third of the land is permanently frozen, and temperatures in Moscow regularly fall to –20C or below in January, but often reach 30C in the summer. The Russian landscape is spectacular – there are huge forests and vast lakes, but reaching this largely unspoilt wilderness can be difficult and time-consuming.

Transport
There are major international airports in Moscow and St Petersburg; these provide regular international and internal flights. Travel by train can be slow and uncomfortable, as the infrastructure is poor. Buses, trams, and especially metros, provide a cheap and effective means of transport. *Marshrutki* (private minibuses) are quicker and more comfortable than state-run city transport, and you're practically guaranteed a seat.

Health arrangements

Emergency treatment is free of charge, but medication has to be paid for, which can make illness or injury expensive, so you should take out insurance. Treatment for foreigners is provided in private medical centres, with services and standards matching those in the UK. Annual insurance costs around US$100.

Higher education

Russia has over 3 million students enrolled in over 880 higher education institutions, including 552 that are state-run. A large number of these institutions have agreements with institutions in the UK. Universities are particularly strong in science and technical engineering subjects, as well as in mathematics, international relations, law, economics and medicine.

Teaching is in Russian, and students need to be proficient to be effective in their studies. Russia's universities are in the process of changing their education system to four years for a Bachelor degree, but some still operate the old five-year system. You should check carefully which programmes are taught in English, as this varies considerably.

History of accepting foreign students

The Soviet Union has a history of welcoming students from around the world for degree studies, usually at no cost. Russian universities are entering a period of domestic competition for students and this is making facilities and teaching conditions better.

Fees

Tuition fees vary widely, depending on the course and institution as well as other items such as accommodation and materials. Foreign students may receive state scholarships to cover some of these costs.

Working while studying

It's possible to work while studying, but you need to be covered by your visa. For charity work or teaching, wages are not high but accommodation is often included, either in your own flat or with a family.

Application/visa system

Potential exchange students should contact the international office of their home institution. For independent students, course applications are made directly to the institution before 1 April. On acceptance you'll need to pass a language examination, or enrol in a one-year preparatory course to gain proficiency.

To study in Russia you'll need a student visa. For those receiving a state scholarship, the visa and other formalities are taken care of usually by the Ministry for Education; fee-paying students should apply through their own university. Visa applications should be accompanied by a negative HIV/AIDS test certificate that's been issued within the last four weeks. When you're in Russia, you'll need to register your passport at the local OVIR (Aliens Registration) office. The Consular Section of the Russian Embassy can help you with any queries on visas.

Expenses/costs
Degree study can range from US$1,500 to $8,000 per year, with other costs (accommodation, food, books, etc) ranging from US$1,500 to $5,000 a year, depending on location and lifestyle.

Accommodation/assistance
Student accommodation in halls is available and generally preferred by foreign students. Rooms are usually shared with one or two other people, although single rooms and apartments are available. Rates for rooms vary according to facilities, size, etc and cost between US$50 and $200 monthly.

Private accommodation is also a viable option. Prices can vary considerably depending on location, quality and levels of security. It's also possible to live with a Russian family.

Academic year
This runs in two semesters, September–December and February–June or July.

Support network
You will need to be resilient, determined and independent to benefit fully from studying in Russia, especially on a full-time basis. A support network has developed in recent years. The main point of contact is the international office, which can help you with practical and academic queries. Many universities also have clubs and associations offering leisure activities.

Volume/type of work
The workload depends on subject discipline. There are likely to be examinations in most subjects, with a relatively small amount of coursework and project-based assignments – this is gradually changing. Expect to spend a lot of time and effort learning Russian.

Useful addresses/websites
British Council Moscow
VGBIL
Ul. Nikoloyamska 1
Moscow 109189
Russia
Tel: (+7) 095 234 0201
Fax: (+7) 095 975 2561

Email: bc.moscow@bc-moscow.sprint.com
Website: www.britishcouncil.ru/ondex.htm

Embassy of the Russian Federation
13 Kensington Palace Gardens
London W8 4QX
Tel: 020 7229 3628
Fax: 020 7727 7281
Website: www.russialink.org.uk/embassy/embassyI

Embassy of the Russian Federation
Consular Department (Visa Applications)
5 Kensington Palace Gardens
London W8 4QX
Tel: 020 7229 8027
Fax: 020 7229 3215
Website: as for Embassy above.

Ministry of Education for the Russian Federation
Ul. Lusinivskaia 51
Moscow 113933
Russia
Tel: (+7) 095 237 7875
Fax: (+7) 095 230 2145
Website: www.ed.gov.ru

Case study 1
St Petersburg State University

Background

Founded in 1724 by Peter the Great, this is the oldest university
in Russia. It has an excellent reputation in science, education and
culture, and has around 100 agreements with universities in 50
countries, including several in the UK. The achievements of St
Petersburg's professors and graduates include eight Nobel Prizes.

Structure

Over 25,000 students, including around 1,500 international
students. There are 20 faculties, from natural sciences to international relations, and 12 specialist research institutes. You can choose
from the full range of academic disciplines here, and many faculties
have good international links. Fees in 2003–4 ranged from
US$2,000–3,000 for a Bachelor's degree, to US$4,000–5,000 for a
specialist degree. Check with the international office for full details.

Social life

There's lots to do in modern St Petersburg – apart from all the activities on campus, there are churches, theatres, galleries and museums, Western-style shops, cinemas, bars, cafes and clubs. There are royal palaces in picturesque forest locations not far from the city, and you can take weekend trips (requiring a re-entry visa) to neighbouring countries: Estonia, Finland, Latvia and Lithuania.

Application/accommodation

International students should apply direct to the university before 30 June for courses starting in the autumn semester, or before 1 January for the spring semester. At enrolment you'll need to pass a language test – if this is failed, you're offered a Russian language course, otherwise you have an interview with the faculty to determine the level at which you'll be studying. You must get health insurance cover, either before you leave for Russia or in St Petersburg.

Accommodation can be arranged via the Division for Non-Academic Affairs in one of the student dorms. These tower blocks accommodate up to 5,000 students in 2-bedroom shared apartments. It's possible to arrange your own room, but only if any are spare after demand has been met. A shared room costs US$50 monthly, or US$100–150 with single occupancy.

Contact

Centre for International Exchanges (CIE)
St Petersburg State University
Universitetskaya nab. 7–9
St Petersburg 199034
Russia
Tel: (+7) 812 328 3291
Fax: (+7) 812 325 8739
Email: alla@ae1635.spb.edu
Website: http://www.spbu.ru/eng/education/CIE/

Case study 2
Plekhanov Russian Academy of Economics, Moscow

Background

Founded in 1907, the Plekhanov is the largest business institute in Russia. There are around 13,000 students, including 200 foreign students. It has over 70 partner institutions in 42 countries. Since

1992 the Plekhanov has offered full degree programmes in English, and is part of the European Double Degree system.

Structure

Both theory and practice are used to teach courses. While studying, students are encouraged to apply theory to the work environment through practical placements, and most of the teaching staff are involved in outside business ventures. The Academy offers a two-level system of economic and business education in ten undergraduate faculties. The first level is a three-year full-time Bachelor degree programme in Economics, taken in the General Economics department. The second is a two-year, full-time Masters degree programme in which students develop professional skills, focusing on their chosen field.

Social life

The Plekhanov is located in the centre of Moscow, within walking distance of Red Square and close to major shops, businesses, social and leisure facilities. The international office is the first port of call for the international student. There is a lively student scene with bars and cafes for every taste.

Applications/accommodation

Foreign students are admitted to any of the international business school programmes on a contractual basis after they have passed an interview and entrance tests in English and mathematics. Tuition fees for any of the international business school study programmes are US$6,000 a year. For exchanges go through your home institution initially.

Accommodation is available in two- and three-room shared apartments, varying from US$700–1,500 a year, depending on the facilities. The campus is situated only five minutes away from the main accommodation building.

Contact

Head of International Office
Plekhanov Russian Academy of Economics
Office 649 36
Stremyanny per.,
Moscow 113054
Russia
Tel: (+7) 095 237 8517
Fax: (+7) 095 237 9518
Email: inter@rea.ru
Website: www.rea.ru

Country profile: South Africa

Population
44.8 million. The capital, Pretoria, has a population of 1.1 million.

History/government
Pretoria is the administrative capital, and Cape Town is the seat of government. The Union of South Africa was established in 1910, and the full apartheid regime was established in 1948. In response to this, the African National Congress (ANC) advocated open resistance. In 1961 South Africa became a republic. A government of national unity was elected in April 1994, with Nelson Mandela as president.

Culture, language and lifestyle
Culture in South Africa can mean many things, from the traditional Eurocentric arts to the alternative arts scene and the expansion of traditional art forms. European and traditional cuisine is available. English and Afrikaans used to be the official languages, and nine African languages have been added now. South African English has assimilated many words from other languages and the pronunciation is very different.

Lifestyle is relaxed, centring on sport and outdoor adventure; barbecuing is one of the most popular outdoor activities. The cities are sophisticated, with active cultural life.

Banking system/currency
The rand (R). Most major UK and international banks are well established in South Africa, and ATMs are widely available. Banks are open Mon–Fri, 9am–3.30pm, and on Saturday 9am–11am.

Climate/geography
The climate and landscape is very varied. The coastal zone is low-lying and narrow, giving way to the Drakensberg mountains in the east. Inland there is the Karoo plateau with scrubland and mountains. To the north the Kalahari desert is very hot in summer, but icy in winter. The eastern coastline is lush and tropical, while the south-west has a Mediterranean climate.

Transport
There are regular domestic flights between the main cities. Train services run throughout the country but services are poor, apart from the luxury Blue Train express. Roads are good, and coaches are popular for inter-city travel. Bus services aren't reliable, so in the city it's best to take a taxi, either a standard taxi or a 'black taxi' (privately owned minibuses covering a wide area, following a particular route).

Health arrangements

Student health services are usually available on campus as part of the student welfare system, but you're advised to take out medical insurance.

Higher education

There are 21 public universities, 15 *technikons* (technical institutes) and many colleges. Universities offer Bachelor's degrees which usually take three years to complete, and specialised honours degrees lasting a further one year.

History of accepting foreign students

Major South African universities welcome foreign students.

Fees

International students have to pay full tuition fees. These vary between institutions and courses, but students can expect to pay between R5,000 and R25,000 annually. There are also application fees of between R70 and R250.

Working while studying

Students are allowed to work while studying, taking into account as always the demands of their course.

Application system/visas

International students have to meet entrance requirements: those without South African matriculation need to get an exemption certificate from the Matriculation Board, showing that their overseas qualifications are equivalent; some faculties also have their own requirements. Students also need to show appropriate language proficiency. You apply direct to the institution.

Once an offer has been made, you'll need to get a study permit from the South African Embassy (a fee is payable and you'll need to renew it annually).

Expenses/costs

The cost of study can vary between institution and region. Budget for around R2,675 a month (this includes accommodation and food).

Accommodation/assistance

This varies from institution to institution. Some offer places in hostels on campus, while for others you may have to rent privately. Help with transport can sometimes be provided as security is a constant concern. The international office can give you advice.

Academic year
This runs in four semesters: February–April, April–June, July–September and September–October.

Support network
All South African universities have a support network called Student Services or Student Support, covering everything from study problems to personal difficulties.

Volume/type of work
Generally heavy – this depends on the type of institution and course, but on the whole, South African universities are moving towards a mixture of the academic and practical, and away from work of a heavily theoretical, academic kind.

Useful addresses/websites
South African High Commission
South Africa House
Trafalgar Square
London WC2N 5DP
Tel: 020 7451 7299
Fax: 020 7451 7284
Email: general@southafrica.com
Website: www.southafricahouse.com

South African Qualifications Authority
Postnet Suite 248
Private Bag X06
Waterkloof 0145
South Africa
Tel: (+27) 12 482 0858
Fax: (+27) 12 431 5039
Email: saqain@saqa.org.za
Website: www.saqa.org.za

Study South Africa Partnership
International Education Association of South Africa
PO Box 65099
Reservoir Hills
Durban 4090
South Africa
Tel: (+27) 31 260 3077
Fax: (+27) 21 650 5667
Email: iapo@world.uct.ac.za
Website: www.studysa.co.za

Case study 1
University of Cape Town

Background

Founded in 1829 as South Africa College, the University of Cape Town became South Africa's first university in 1918 and is now one of the leading higher education institutions in the country. It's located in the peaceful suburb of Rondebosch, about 10 minutes' drive from the city centre; the main campus is on the slopes of Table Mountain.

Structure

There are six faculties: humanities; science; law; engineering and the built environment; commerce; health sciences. Humanities include schools of drama, dance and music. The student population in 2002 was around 18,985, including 2,500 international students. The teaching language is English.

Social life

There's an exciting range of sporting and other activities, including paragliding, skydiving, snowskiing, waterskiing and scuba diving. There are over 60 societies run by students, with cultural activities including theatre and an opera school.

Application/accommodation

Details on exchange programmes are on the university website (www.uct.ac.za); to apply, contact your own institution. International students wanting to take full degrees should contact the International Academic Programme Office (IAPO). You need to obtain an exemption certificate from South African matriculation, and to check on faculty demands.

There's a limited amount of accommodation for international students on campus. Special arrangements are available for under-21-year-olds in catered accommodation with a warden on-site. The Student Accommodation Office (SAO) can give you more information. Most students share houses off-campus – lists are available from the Student Housing and IAPO. IAPO also acts as a central contact point for international students and runs the Semester Study Abroad Programme.

Contact

International Academic Programme Office
University of Cape Town
Private Bag

Rondebosch 7701
South Africa
Tel: (+27) 21 650 2822
Fax: (+27) 21 650 5667
Email: iapo@world.za
Website: www.uct.ac.za

Case study 2
University of Pretoria

Background
Founded in 1908 as a branch of the Transvaal University College,
the University of Pretoria came into being in 1930. It now has
55,000 students.

Structure
There are nine faculties: economic and management sciences;
engineering, the built environment and IT; health sciences;
natural and agricultural sciences; veterinary sciences; education;
humanities; law; theology. Teaching is in English and Afrikaans.

Social life
There's a wide range of interests catered for including a symphony
orchestra, student choirs and a film festival. Over 50 associations
provide activities. University of Pretoria International (UPI)
welcomes both international and home students, with trips,
cultural events and an international day. Sport is well provided
for.

Application/accommodation
If you plan to study in Pretoria through an exchange, your university will make most of the arrangements. For independent
students, the first step is to make sure that you have appropriate
qualifications, and minimum faculty requirements must also be
met (see above for details, and contact the Admissions Office).

Accommodation is provided in hostels. These each have their
own character: some cater for students from specific courses or for
specifically English- or Afrikaans-speaking students. They run
their own sports and cultural events and have a house father or
mother in charge. You can apply direct to the hostel when the
university has offered you a place.

Contact
Admissions Office
University of Pretoria
Pretoria 0002
South Africa
Tel: (+27) 12 420 4111
Fax: (+27) 12 362 5168
Email: clientservice@postino.up.ac.za
Website: www.up.ac.za

Country Profile: Spain

Population
40 million. The capital, Madrid, has a population of 3.5 million.

History/government
Spain has a long, complex history. For centuries it ruled a vast empire in Central and South America. More recently, the consequences of a divisive civil war in the 1930s meant that Spain spent almost 40 years under the Franco dictatorship, until 1975. Spain joined the EC (now EU) in 1986.

Culture, language and lifestyle
The difference in Spanish culture is really expressed in its languages. Most people speak and understand Castilian Spanish, although regional languages are widely used in universities, the media and at work in the independent regions of Spain. These are Basque in the north-west, Catalan in the north-east and Gallego in the far north-west.

Spanish life is influenced by the climate. The afternoon siesta is a key feature, when shops and businesses close. Football is an all-consuming passion, and bullfighting remains popular. Spanish cuisine celebrates seafood (especially paella) and good wine.

Banking system/currency
The euro (€). Banking hours are Monday–Friday, 8.30am–2pm. ATMs are widely available.

Climate/geography
Spain is a mountainous country with six major ranges. It has a varied climate. The central area (around Madrid) is hot and dry in summer but cold in winter, while the south has a Mediterranean climate. The northern coast has a lot of rainfall.

Transport
Several low-cost airlines fly regularly from the UK – internal flights tend to be expensive. The major airports are Madrid, Barcelona El Prat, Alicante and Malaga. Good rail connections run between major cities, and fares are reasonable; journeys can be slow in the mountain areas. Bus and coach travel can be both faster and cheaper.

Health arrangements
You should take form E111 with you to Spain. All EU students (under 28 years) who are registered at a university or higher education institution are automatically included in the Spanish Student Health Scheme, which provides cover for primary health care and other services.

Higher education

The Bachelor's degree (*Licenado*) usually takes between four and six years to complete, depending on your field of study. UK nationals have the right to study full-time in Spain, but you need to think carefully about this. The cost and length of courses means that it's more likely that you'll go under the Erasmus/Socrates exchange programme.

History of accepting foreign students

Spain welcomes international students and attracts many from Latin America. There are well-developed exchange links between Spanish and UK universities.

Fees

Individual institutions set the level of tuition and registration fees on an annual basis varying between €607–1,414 annually, depending on the course. Details of exact fees from the institution concerned.

Working while studying

May be possible in the tourist areas but unemployment is high and you'll need good spoken Spanish.

Application system/visas

Exchange students should contact their home institution. Almost all courses are in Spanish, so you'll need a competent level of written and spoken Spanish (some courses may also include a second official language, such as Basque or Gallego). Most Spanish universities offer language and cultural studies courses specifically for international/ exchange students.

For full time study, apply direct to your chosen institution as early as possible in the year before you plan to go (you apply for more than one course with order of preference). EU and Spanish students' applications are usually treated equally. For more information, contact the international office at your chosen institution.

UK nationals don't require study permits or a visa, but you'll need to get a study visa from the Spanish Embassy before you leave if you plan to live and study full-time in Spain for more than three months. You must also show proof that you've been accepted on a course and that you've got financial support. Within 90 days of arrival in Spain, be sure to apply at the local police station for a student card (renewed annually).

Expenses/costs

Budget for a minimum of €379 monthly to cover living and travel expenses. It's not a good idea to consider studying full-time in Spain unless you've got access to enough finance to cover all of your studies.

Accommodation/assistance

Accommodation is arranged via the international office of the university – you can either live in halls (the earlier you apply, the better) or private accommodation. Costs range from €450–861 monthly, depending on facilities and location. Cities such as Madrid and Barcelona are more expensive.

Academic year

This runs from September/October–January, and February–June, in two semesters.

Support network

In addition to the international and Socrates offices, student organisations are beginning to develop sporting, cultural and political groups – these can help you to adapt to living and studying in Spain.

Volume/type of work

Most Spanish universities are rooted in academic tradition, so (with a few exceptions), there is a lot of theory in study programmes, although this is slowly starting to change. You can expect to be in large lectures for most subjects, and to read and study independently. Assessment is generally by way of examination, though there is also coursework, project work and presentations in some subjects.

Useful addresses/websites

Spanish Embassy
39 Chesham Place
London SW1X 2PZ
Tel: 0870 005 6975
Fax: 020 7235 9905
Website: www.mcx.es/londres

Case study 1
Universidade de Santiago de Compostela
(University of Santiago de Compostela)

Background

Founded in 1494, the University was one of the earliest in Europe. It's mostly located in the medieval city, although there's also a campus in Lugo Santiago. Over the centuries it has built up a reputation for academic excellence and as a centre promoting and preserving Galician language, folklore and traditions. The city is a religious centre, a destination for pilgrims who flock to its magnificent cathedral each year.

Structure

A public university with 19 faculties, together with a small number of schools. There are approximately 40,000 full-time students. The university takes part in a wide range of international projects with partner institutions in Europe and beyond. The External Relations Office is the first port of call in Santiago for prospective full-time and exchange students.

Social life

Living and studying in Galicia has its own distinctive character – Santiago has many cafes, restaurants and bars; seafood is a speciality. As a university town, there's plenty to do through clubs and societies. Galicia is green and fertile, with Celtic music and traditions; it's a good idea to spend time travelling in the region itself, from its dramatic coast to its small villages and towns.

Applications/accommodation

Potential exchange students should contact the international office of their home institution. If you're considering full-time study, you should apply directly to the faculty concerned – the international office will help you with this. Click on the information/services link on the website for more details. Although the university is developing its international dimension, you'll need to learn Spanish and be open to Galician.

Accommodation is either in halls or private housing, and it's cheaper than the UK – the accommodation office will help you. You need to apply for halls well in advance. Private accommodation is usually cheaper, and it's commonplace for exchange/international students to stay in pensions (bed & breakfast) for a few days after arrival. The accommodation office can give you a list of available places on request.

Contact

External Relations Office
Colexio de San Xerome
Universidade de Santiago de Compostela
Plaza de Obradoires
15782 Santiago de Compostela
Spain
Tel: (+34) 981 584989
Fax: (+34) 981 573017
Email: elveloso@usc.es
Website: http://www.usc.es/intro/benvidai.htm

Case study 2
Universidad de Navarra, Pamplona (University of Navarra, Pamplona)

Background

Founded in 1952 by St José-Maria Escriba de Balaguer, this private university was committed to the Catholic Church's philosophy of *Opus Dei* – a pastoral environment in which to live and study. The main, modern campus is just outside the city of Pamplona in northern-central Spain, although the university also has business schools in Barcelona and Madrid. Pamplona itself is most famous for the bull run in July each year, attracting thousands of visitors from Spain and overseas.

Structure

There are 10 faculties divided into several schools and departments, offering 27 undergraduate programmes to approximately 15,000 full-time students. There is a well-developed international dimension to studying in Pamplona – with the university involved in more than 250 partnerships with other European institutions. Good support system exists for international/exchange students via the Service for International Relations.

Social life

This mostly revolves around Pamplona's well-preserved old town, with many bars, cafes and restaurants close to the central Plaza de Castillo. Everything's within walking distance, especially if you happen to live in or close to the old quarter itself, which is full of character. Seafood and tapas is popular and inexpensive. Pamplona itself has good bus and rail connections with most of the other regions of Spain.

Applications/accommodation

For exchanges, contact the international office of your home institution.

For full-time study, apply directly to the Registry. You'll need to satisfy basic entry conditions (check the website for details), including a proficiency in Spanish.

The accommodation office in Pamplona can help you – it's possible to rent a room in halls on campus (the accommodation link on the website gives you some ideas as to cost), but you're advised to apply for a place well in advance. You can also rent inexpensive private accommodation in Pamplona, in either the old or new town. It's worth staying in a pension for a few days after you arrive

– the university can help you with this and to find a more permanent place to live.

Contact
The Registry
University of Navarra, Pamplona
31080 Pamplona
Spain
Tel: (+34) 948 425600
Fax: (+34) 948 425619
Email: mbainfo@iese.es
Website: http://www.unav.es/english/

Country profile: Sweden

Population
8.87 million. The capital, Stockholm, has a population of 2 million.

History/government
Very much shaped by its relationship with its Scandinavian neighbours, with traditional territorial disputes with Norway and Denmark. More recently noted for its political neutrality. Sweden joined the EU in 1995.

Culture, language and lifestyle
In keeping with the climate, winter sports (including ice skating and skiing) are popular, as are cycling and canoeing. The official language is Swedish, but English is widely spoken, especially in the major cities. Seafood is popular, served with potatoes, and cuisine in the main cities is more cosmopolitan. The beer is also excellent, if expensive.

Banking system/currency
The Swedish krona (K). Banks are generally open from Monday–Friday, 9.30am–3pm. Many branches have extended opening hours at least once a week (until 6pm in larger cities). ATMs are widely available.

Climate/geography
Temperate in the south with cold, cloudy winters and cool summers. In the north it's sub-arctic with bitterly cold winters and cool summers. The land is densely forested with many lakes and flat or gently rolling lowlands; the west is mountainous. The midnight sun can be seen between mid-May and mid-June above the Arctic Circle, giving spectacular views.

Transport
There are international airports at Stockholm and Gothenburg, with regular flights to most major European destinations. Internal travel by air is relatively cheap and efficient. There is also an extensive train and bus system. Trains are the basis of transport outside cities, serving regional centres quickly. Buses are often the only option off the beaten track, especially in the far north.

Health arrangements
Form E111 entitles you to emergency medical treatment on the same terms as Swedish nationals. However, you may feel that health insurance is a useful precaution.

Higher education
The oldest universities, Uppsala and Lund, were established in the 15th

and 17th centuries respectively. Today, approximately 300,000 students follow undergraduate programmes at universities and colleges. Higher education is government-funded and, with a few exceptions, there are no tuition fees for Swedish or foreign students. This makes Sweden a viable option for study, especially if you're interested in a course that's mostly taught in English – although you will still need to learn Swedish for full-time study.

History of accepting foreign students
Some 20 per cent are from non-Swedish backgrounds. The most common way for students from the UK to study in Sweden is via the Erasmus/Socrates programme. Many courses are taught in English (check this with your home university). Swedish universities tend to be very proactive in this area, and have well-established collaborative programmes. UK nationals can study full-time and are treated in the same way as Swedish nationals.

Fees
With rare exceptions, higher education tuition fees in Sweden are fully subsidised by the government. Scholarships aren't awarded by higher education institutions, but the Swedish Institute does have a limited number. Students have to pay a small membership fee to the local student union (K150–400 each term).

Working while studying
You can work throughout the academic year and no work permit is necessary. If you do get a job, even if it's only for a short period, you'll need to register with your local tax office. The address is under *Skattemyndigheten* in the telephone directory (you will not be liable for tax if you earn less than K8,700).

Application system/visas
Students interested in exchanges should initially contact the international office at their own institution. Independent applications to first degree and single subject courses are made via the National Agency for Higher Education (VHS) – the deadline is 1 December for courses in the following academic year. Application forms are available from VHS, the Swedish Embassy, or directly from the institution of your choice. The applications need to be sent to the Swedish Embassy in your own country.

UK citizens don't need a visa or permit to stay. However, if you intend to study full-time, you must register with the local police, and if you're staying longer than three months, you must obtain a residence permit.

Expenses/costs
Budget for between €810 and €876 monthly for food, transport, health

insurance and accommodation. The cost of living in Stockholm and Gothenburg is more expensive.

Accommodation/assistance
If you're an exchange student, you'll get help with accommodation from the host university. Be sure to confirm this with your contact person before you leave for Sweden. If you're a prospective full-time student, all applications must be made directly to the student union at your chosen institution. The accommodation situation is difficult in larger cities, especially in Stockholm and Gothenburg.

Academic year
This is run in two semesters, September–January and January–June.

Support network
The student union has a large number of societies where you can meet people who share your interests, and is the focal point for practical and welfare support together with leisure activities. International offices are usually well organised and very helpful.

Volume/type of work
Much of this depends on the subject you've chosen, and teaching ranges from large scale lectures to individual tutorials. You'll usually spend between 8 and 11 hours a week in class, although you're expected to do a lot of independent study – up to 40 hours per week. Classes of 20–30 students are common. For most courses you'll complete a mixture of essays, projects and examinations (these can be written or oral).

Useful addresses/websites
Swedish Embassy
11 Montagu Place
London W1H 2AL
Tel: 020 7917 8400
Fax: 020 7917 6475
Email: ambasseden.london@foreign.ministry.se
Website: www.swedish-embassy.org.uk/

Swedish Institute
Box 7434
10391 Stockholm
Sweden
Tel: (+46) 0 878 92000
Fax: (+46) 0 870 72480
Email: si@si.se
Website: www.si.se

VHS (National Agency for Higher Education)
Box 12615
Drottningholmsvagen 37
11292 Stockholm
Sweden
Tel: (+46) 0 872 59600
Fax: (+46) 0 872 59600
Email: registrator@vhs.se
Website: www.vhs.se

Case study 1
Göteborgs Universitet (University of Gothenburg)

Background
Most of the university is situated in the city centre, so it plays a key role in the cultural and educational life of the city as a whole.

Structure
Six faculties split up into almost 70 departments, offering the most comprehensive range of courses and degree programmes in Sweden. The university has about 40,000 students, giving a real campus atmosphere. It has an excellent record for research.

Social life
Gothenburg has a rich and varied cultural life with many theatres, concerts, festivals, an art museum and annual film festival. Liseberg is the biggest theme park in the Nordic area. For outdoor life, forests and vast recreation areas are nearby, and the sea is within easy reach.

Admissions/accommodation
The Admissions Office deals with all aspects of the admissions process. Apply for courses by 15 April for the autumn term, and 15 October for the spring term. There are some courses in English, and exchange agreements with a number of colleges and universities around the world.

International Exchange Student Services arranges accommodation for incoming exchange students, provided their applications are submitted well in advance of the deadline. All non-exchange international students arrange their own accommodation. Many international students live at SGS (check www.sgsbostader.com for full details of these facilities).

Contact
Admissions Office
Göteborgs Universitet
Box 150 (Karl Gustavsgatan 29)
40530 Göteborg
Sweden
Tel: (+46) 031 773 1855
Fax: (+46) 031 773 4387
Email: antagning@adm.gu.se
Website: www.gu.se

Case study 2
Högskolen i Skövde (University of Skövde)

Background
With a population of 50,000 Skövde is one of the largest towns in the region of Västra Götalands Iän. The university was established in 1977 and is expanding rapidly. The campus is in the town centre.

Structure
There are currently approximately 5,000 students in nine departments ranging from computer science to languages. Most of the courses are taught in Swedish, so be careful to check which departments offer programmes in English. There are growing links with international partners (some in the UK), and the international office is very helpful.

Social life
Skövde's position gives you access to different sports and other activities. It's only a two-hour drive to the west coast, and Europe's two largest lakes are only 30 minutes away. There's also a range of cultural activities, cinemas, theatres, an art museum, about 30 restaurants and many pubs.

Applications/accommodation
Exchange students should approach their home university in the first instance for an application form (academic records and a CV must also be submitted). The deadline for the autumn semester (for courses in English) is 15 May, for the spring semester, 15 October. For courses in Swedish, the deadline for the autumn semester is 15 April, and for the spring semester, 15 October.

If your university doesn't have an exchange programme with Skövde, contact the international coordinator at your university so that you can make a formal request to the International Relations Office to be accepted as a non-exchange student. Deadlines are as for Swedish courses above.

Your letter of acceptance will include a student accommodation offer. If you return it by the deadline, you'll be guaranteed a furnished room costing approximately K2,500 inclusive. It's a good idea to budget for around K6,500 monthly.

Contact
University of Skövde
Högskolevägen
PO Box 408
54128 Skövde
Sweden
Tel: (+46) 500 448000
Fax: (+46) 500 416325
Email: info@his.se
Website: http://www.his.se/his/welcome_eng.htm

Case study: Switzerland

Population
7.3 million. The capital, Bern, has a population of 0.9 million.

History/government
Switzerland became a country in 1848 as a number of areas (cantons) federated to complete a process that began in 1291. Each area still has a high degree of independence. The president is head of state and there is a federal assembly.

Culture, language and lifestyle
There are four national languages: German, French, Italian and Romansh. The Swiss have in common a preference for efficiency, punctuality and cleanliness which makes life easy for travellers, but the French-speaking western part of Switzerland has a very different atmosphere from the German-speaking north, or the Italianate Ticino. Culture, food and attitude are all different. Food is expensive, but high-quality.

Lifestyle varies considerably between regions. Each canton tries to keep its individual character. City life in Geneva and Zürich is sophisticated and expensive, while to the south of the Alps the Italianate style is more relaxed, if equally expensive. As well as being venues for summer and winter sports, the Alpine regions are agricultural, wild and remote.

Banking system/currency
The Swiss franc (SFr). Banking hours are usually from Monday–Friday, 8.30am–2.30pm. ATMs are widely available.

Climate/geography
Much of Switzerland is mountainous, with the high Alps lying towards the south and east. To the north lies a region of hills, lakes and a few high mountains. The Suisse-Romande is in the west with Lake Geneva; the Ticino, south of the Alps, combines Italianate lakeside towns and sub-tropical flora with mountain scenery. The climate is equally varied. South of the Alps it is quite mild, with very hot summers. To the north, the climate is typical of western Europe.

Transport
This is integrated, punctual and efficient. The main airports are Basel, Zürich and Geneva. The train network covers much of the country, apart from mountainous areas (the Postbus service operates in these regions). In the towns and cities there are reliable trams and buses. Ferries operate on all the larger lakes.

Health arrangements

There is no reciprocal agreement with the UK for health services. Form E111 isn't valid and medical expenses can be very high, so you should get insurance before you go to Switzerland. Any costs must be paid by the individual or through insurance.

Higher education

Each canton is responsible for its own system so there are variations between areas. There are 12 official higher education establishments and a number of colleges as well as the new universities of applied sciences. There are also a number of private institutions. Courses leading to a first qualification are generally four or five years in length.

History of accepting foreign students

Swiss universities have always welcomed foreign students, but the high cost of living and need to pay full fees can be deterrents to studying there. As Switzerland isn't a full partner in the Erasmus/Socrates programme, it's difficult to arrange exchanges, but there are alternatives. The universities do have a full programme of international cooperation in research and teaching.

Fees

Tuition fees vary between SFr1,000 and SFr2,000 annually.

Working while studying

It's very difficult to get permission to work while studying. Requests for a vacation work permit must go to the rectorate of the university, but they're not always granted. Universities have offices that help with employment advice.

Application system/visas

As an independent student you should apply directly to your chosen university. You'll need to have the equivalent of the Swiss *Matura* qualification and a good knowledge of the language. If your qualifications aren't accepted then you may have to take an entrance examination, which is held in Fribourg. If you're offered a place, you should apply to the Swiss Embassy for a residence permit.

Expenses/costs

Annual living costs are estimated at SFr16,000.

Accommodation/assistance

Swiss universities don't provide student accommodation, but they do have accommodation offices that can help you to find somewhere to live. There are many student housing associations and cooperatives running student housing complexes, as well as private rooms and apartments. All accommodation is expensive.

Academic year
This runs in two semesters, October–March and April–July.

Support network
All major universities have a range of support and advice services to help students, whether academic or personal.

Volume/type of work
Overall, the volume of work is heavy with regular examination sessions. Work is generally highly academic. Assessment can be by examination, presentation of papers or research projects.

Useful addresses/websites
Central Office of the Swiss Universities
Sennweg 2
3012 Bern
Switzerland
Tel: (+41) 31 306 60 44
Fax: (+41) 21 692 20 15
Email: uniscope@unil.ch
Website: www.crus.ch

Case study
Université de Lausanne (University of Lausanne)

Background
Founded in 1537 as a school of theology, the original institution grew steadily until it became a university in 1890. The vast main site is now on the north shore of Lake Geneva, on terraces rising above the lake. Lausanne is easily accessible, being at the centre of a key road and rail network.

Structure
Seven faculties with 10,000 students including many from abroad. While the University doesn't participate in the Erasmus/Socrates programme, it does pursue a policy of international collaboration at all levels, including student exchanges. The teaching language is generally French. Classes are provided for non-native speakers, but proof of competence is needed.

Social life

Cultural and artistic events happen often, particularly the Grange of Dorigny: university theatre festival, exhibitions, concerts and much more. There are many student societies providing activities from cinema to sport, and the city is buzzing with life and energy. Lausanne's location makes for a lively social life, from sailing and swimming to cross-country skiing, clubs, bars and cafes.

Applications/accommodation

Potential exchange students should contact their own institution to see if any suitable exchanges are organised with Lausanne. Independent students should contact the Admissions Department – generally, they're required to have at minimum the equivalent of the Swiss *Matura* certificate and proof of language competence.

The university doesn't have any student accommodation but the Central Housing Service will help you in your search: student housing foundations have rooms or apartments that can be shared. The service is based in the Socio-cultural Affairs Department, which also helps students to look for work. Advice on personal problems or medical matters can also be had here.

Contact

Admissions Department (Bureau des immatriculations et inscriptions)
Université de Lausanne
UNIL-BRA
1015 Lausanne
Switzerland
Tel: (+41) 021 692 21 00
Email: immat@immat.unil.ch
Website: www.unil.ch/immat

Country profile: USA

Population
270 million.

History/government
The USA is a federal country with individual states having responsibilities for their own higher education provision, although a lively private sector also functions.

Culture, language and lifestyle
US culture and food varies considerably from area to area and coast to coast. Lifestyle varies a lot, depending where you're based. The cities can be vibrant and exhilarating, but also possibly threatening (for example, New York has taken great steps to clean up its image recently). The rural areas can seem quite provincial.

Banking system/currency
The US dollar (US$). The banking system is similar to the UK's, but many banks are regionally based.

Climate/geography
Climate varies across time zones, so check climatic conditions in the area you plan to visit.

Health arrangements
Health care in the USA is not free of charge – you must have adequate insurance or cover before you go.

Higher education
This is administered by each state, each having its own state and other universities; there are also many private universities. The best universities in the USA rank amongst the best in the world, but there are huge variations lower down the scale. Degrees tend to take four years, but they're based on a credit system, so the length can be extended. Content is more general than the UK, and is based on major and minor subjects.

History of accepting foreign students
The Institute of International Education recently estimated that international students spend US$7billion annually on their education in the USA – so this is a large part of the system. There's been continuing yearly growth for some time, but there are recent signs of a slowdown.

Fees
Vary enormously according to the course and the prestige of the institution – from around US$4,000 up to US$40,000 a year.

Working while studying
Students on an F1 visa are allowed to work on campus for 20 hours a week (subject to approval by the institution). For visa purposes, off-campus work can't be listed as contributing towards income (i.e. proof of financial stability).

Application features/visas
Entry requirements are the same as for the UK, but you may have to take either the American College Testing Programme or the Scholastics Achievement Test (SAT) 1. There's no centralised clearing system, so you'll need to apply direct to the university (you may have to pay a fee). Each university has its own closing date (usually around six months before the course starts).

You'll require a valid visa prior to entry and the university will send you the appropriate documentation. You then deal via the US Embassy – you'll need payment, proof of your financial situation and passport to get an F1 or J1 visa.

Expenses/costs
Vary widely from around US$6,000 to US$16,000 with books at US$500 per semester. Many universities have partial scholarships (these are unlikely to cover your full costs – see the Fulbright Commission library). There are also partial sports scholarships at many universities. All scholarships are annual, but can be renewed for up to four years.

Support network
All universities have full support systems.

Volume/type of work
This is similar to the UK, although the emphasis on the type of work will vary according to the course of study and the nature of the institution.

Useful addresses/websites
American Embassy
24 Grosvenor Square
London W1A 1AE
Tel: 020 7499 9000
Website: www.usembassy.org.uk
College Prospects of America, Inc
PO Box 269
Logan, OH 43138–029

USA
Tel: (001) 740 385 6624
Fax: (001) 740 385 9065
Email: homeoffice@cpoa.com
Website: www.cpoa.com

Fulbright Commission
Education Advisory Service
Fulbright House
62 Doughty Street
London WC1N 2JZ
Tel: 020 7404 6994
Fax: 020 7404 6874
Email: education@fulbright.co.uk
Website: www.fulbright.co.uk

Case study 1
University of Southern California (USC)

Background
Founded in 1880, USC is one of the world's leading research universities. It's a private university, located in the heart of Los Angeles.

Structure
USC prides itself on its small class sizes and receives applications from every state in the US, as well as internationally. The university claims that almost 60 per cent of all students receive some form of financial assistance and students likely to have financial problems are encouraged to use work–study plans to help fund themselves (the university has assistance arrangements for this).

Social life
USC has extensive social facilities on campus including highly regarded sports teams, cinemas, theatres, music venues and arts events. You will need a car to get around.

Applications/accommodation
Apply direct to the university through the website instructions. The website also has extensive information about funding arrangements.

USC has extensive student housing, but you need to make your application at an early date (May at the very latest). There are arrangements to link first year students with similar interests.

Interim housing arrangements can be made for international students who don't already have their housing plans arranged. At all stages in the process you'll be required to pay deposits, and actual costs depend upon the type of accommodation (see the housing section of the website: www.usc.edu).

Contact
University of Southern California
University Park Campus
Los Angeles, CA 90089–0914
USA
Tel: (001) 213 740 2311 or 323 442 2000 (for Health Services campus)
Fax: (001) 213 740 2311
Website: www.usc.edu

Case study 2
University of Kansas

Background
Founded in 1864 and based in Lawrence, north-east Kansas, the university is a major research and teaching institution with centres in Kansas City and other cities.

Structure
In the first year, students enter into the College of Liberal Arts & Sciences or the Schools of Engineering, Fine Arts or Architecture and Urban Planning before entering more professional programmes in the Schools of Allied Health, Business, Education, Journalism and Mass Communication, Nursing, Pharmacy or Social Welfare.

Social life
The University has an excellent range of campus-based activities. Lawrence, in northeast Kansas, is a fast-growing, multi-cultural town with a reputation for a lively entertainment and arts scene.

Applications/accommodation
Apply via the online application form on the website (www.apply-web.com/apply/kui/). The fees structure is complex and should be consulted on the website, as should application procedures and eligibility for financial aid.

The university has halls of residence, scholarship halls,

Jayhawker Towers and Stouffer Place (for single-parent and married students, plus spouses and children). Apply direct to the Department of Student Housing.

Contact
ISSS Admissions
Kansas University
4 Strong Hall
1450 Jayhawk Blvd
Lawrence, KS 66045
USA
Tel: (001) 785 864 2616
Fax: (001) 785 864 3404
Website: www.applyweb.com/apply/kui/

Useful Addresses and Publications

Association of Commonwealth Universities
John Foster House
38 Gordon Square
London WC1H 0PF
Tel: 020 7380 6700
Website: www.aca.ac.uk

Careerscope (Careers publisher)
12a Princess Way
Camberley
Surrey GU15 3SP
Tel: 01276 21188
Fax: 01276 691833
Website: www.careerscope.info

College Prospects of America, Inc (advisers on Sports Scholarships)
PO Box 269
Logan, OH 43138–0269
USA
Tel: (001) 740 385 6624
Fax: (001) 740 385 9065
Email: homeoffice@cpoa.com
Website: www.cpoa.com

Department for Education and Skills
Sanctuary Buildings
Great Smith Street
London SW1P 3BT
Tel: 0870 000 2288
Fax: 01928 79448
Email: info@dfes.gsi.gov.uk
Website: www.dfes.gov.uk

The European Commission
8 Storey's Gate
London SW1P 3AT
Tel: 020 7973 1992
Fax: 020 7973 1900
Email: jim.douglas@cec.org.uk
Website: www.cec.org.uk
(see also www.europe.org.uk)
Foreign and Commonwealth Office
King Charles Street

London SW1A 2AH
Tel: 0870 6060 290 (travel enquiries)
or 020 7008 1500 (main switchboard)
Website: www.fco.gov.uk

Fulbright Commission
Education Advisory Service
Fulbright House
62 Doughty Street
London WC1N 2JZ
Tel: 020 7404 6994
Fax: 020 7404 6874
Email: education@fulbright.co.uk
Website: www.fulbright.co.uk

Inland Revenue
National Insurance Contributions Office
International Services
Longbenton
Newcastle-upon-Tyne NE98 1ZZ
Tel: 0845 915 4811
Website: www.inlandrevenue.gov.uk

Irish Council for International Students
41 Morehampton Road
Donneybrook
Dublin 4
Ireland
Tel: (+353) 1 660 5233
Fax: (+353) 1 669 2320
Email: office@iocosirl.ie

ISIS Educational Services
259 Greenwich High Road
London SE10 8NB
Tel: 020 8293 1188
Fax: 020 8293 1199
Email: info@isisgroup.co.uk
Website: www.isisgroup.co.uk

NARIC Ltd (for information on comparability of international
qualification)
Oriel House
Oriel Road
Cheltenham
Gloucestershire GL50 1XP

Tel: 01242 258605
Fax: 01242 258611
Email: customer.services@naric.org.uk
Website: www.naric.org.uk

National Insurance Contributions Office
International Services
Longbenton
Newcastle-upon-Tyne NE98 1ZZ
Tel: 0845 915 4811

Office of the European Parliament
2 Queen Anne's Gate
London SW1H 9AA
Tel: 020 7227 4300
Website: www.europarl.org.uk

Petersons (international education bookseller)
Princeton Pike Corporate Centre
2000 Lennox Drive
PO Box 67005
Lawrenceville NJ 08648
Tel: (001) 609869 1880
Fax: (001) 609 898 1811
Email: custsvc@petersons.com
Website: www.petersons.com

Ploteus (the European Commission's portal providing information on
learning opportunities across Europe)
Email: eac-ploteus@cec.eu.int
Website: www.ploteus.com

Relay Europe (publisher of EU information)
112 Malling Street
Lewes
Sussex BN7 2RJ

Socrates and Youth Technical Assistance Office
70 rue Montoyer
B-1000 Brussels
Belgium
Tel: (+32) 2 233 0111
Fax: (+32) 2 233 0150
Email: info@socrates-youth.be
Website: http://elwa.ilu.uuse/jansju/odette.htm
UCAS
Rosehill

New Barn Lane
Cheltenham
Gloucestershire GL52 3LZ
Tel: 0870 1112211
Email: enquiries@ucas.ac.uk
Website: www.ucas.ac.uk

UK Erasmus/Socrates Council
Research and Development Building
The University
Canterbury
Kent CT2 7PD
Tel: 01227 762712
Fax: 01227 762711
Email: erasmus@ukc.ac.uk
Website: www.ukc.ac.uk/erasmus/erasmus/

Vacation Work Publications
9 Park End Street
Oxford OX1 1HJ
Tel: 01865 241978
Email: sales@vacationwork.co.uk
Website: www.vacationwork.co.uk

Experience Erasmus (£14.95, ISBN 0 901936 87 1).

Commonwealth University Yearbook (published annually by the Association of Commonwealth Universities, £200, ISBN 0 85143 184 4).

Applying to Colleges and Universities in the US.

Sports Scholarships and College Athletic Programs in the US ($26.95, ISBN 0 7689 09273 8).